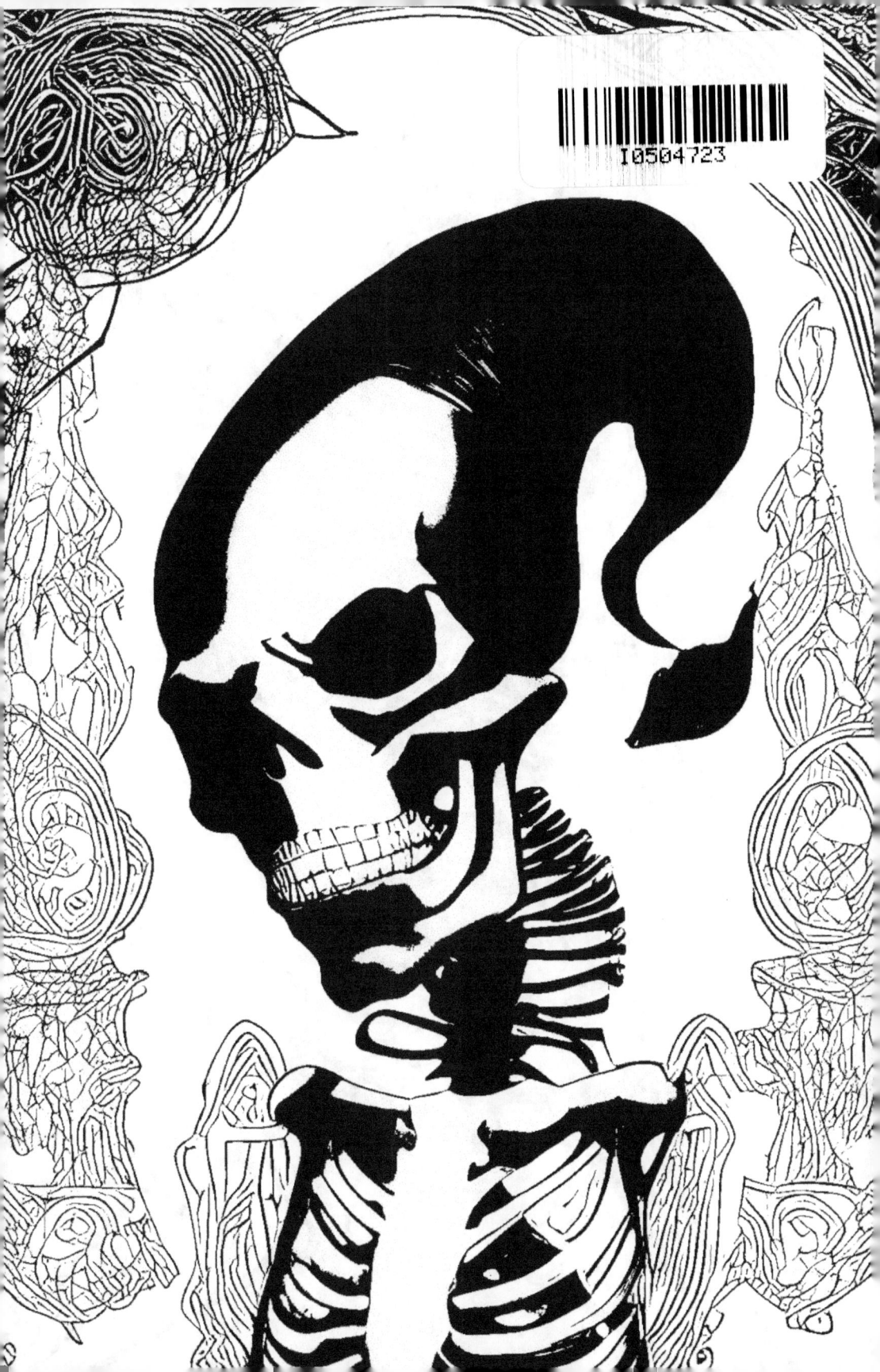

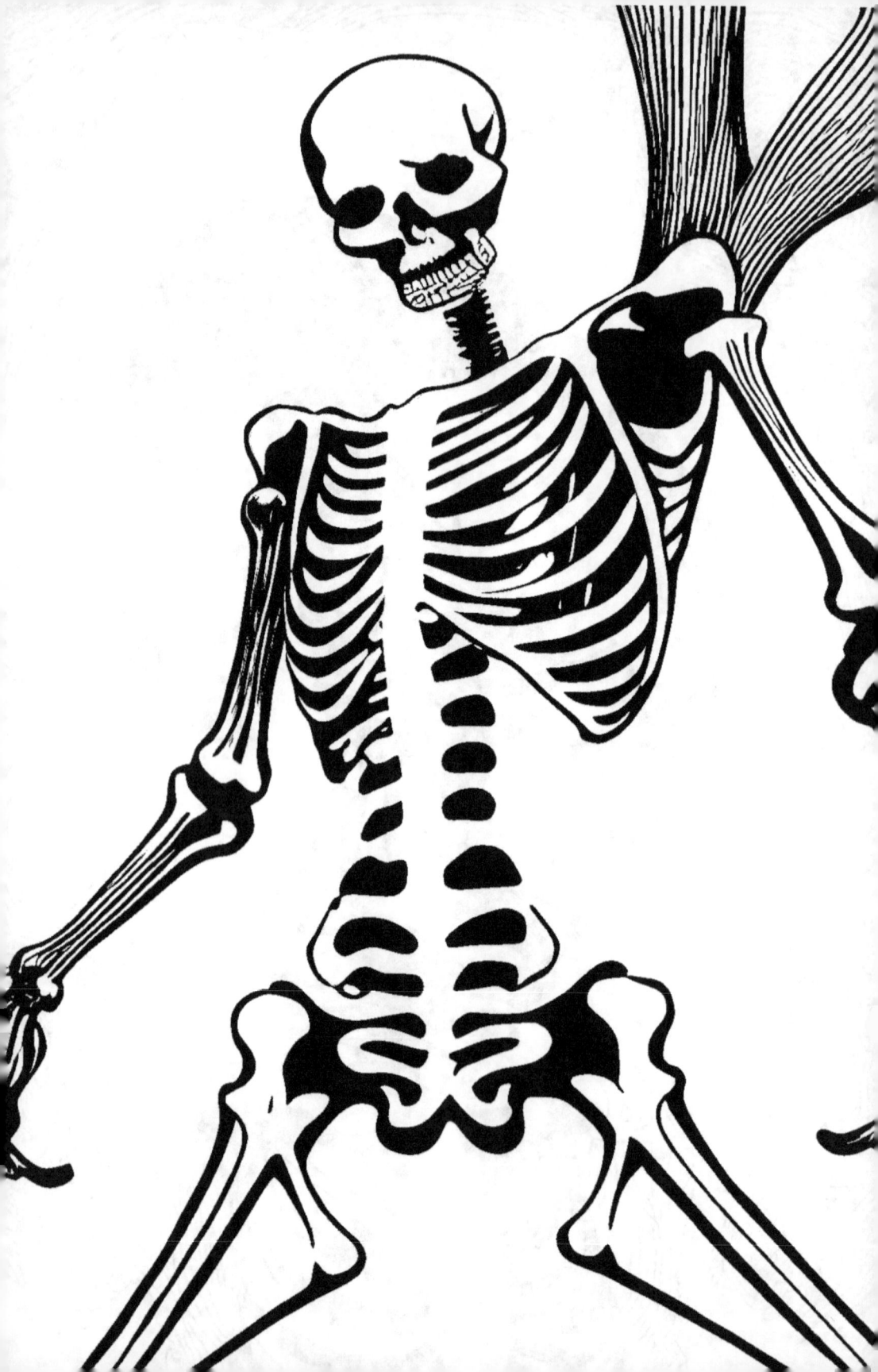

AI SKELETON COLORING BOOK

Hey there, I'm Jeremy Hubert Burt. I was feeling inspired and decided to use a prompt to create some 3D coloring book pages. The prompt I used was:

"Design an intriguing coloring book page featuring a skeleton game character. Against a pristine white background, use bold black lines to illustrate the character's intricate details, creating a sense of mystery and excitement.

Create a dynamic and engaging environment that complements the skeleton character, immersing the viewer in a world of adventure and fantasy. The background designs should evoke a sense of action and intrigue, capturing the imagination.

Incorporate various shapes such as angular lines, swirling patterns, and thematic elements throughout the page, inviting individuals to explore the depths of the character's world. Add bold phrases in a font that captures the essence of excitement and thrill, enhancing the sense of anticipation and discovery.

Outline the character with bold black lines, clearly defining the boundaries for coloring. This allows enthusiasts to bring the skeleton game character to life using their own creativity and imagination, using the striking contrast of black and white.

The coloring book page promises an exciting journey into the realm of the skeleton game character. It invites individuals to engage in the art of coloring, providing a delightful sense of relaxation and stress relief. Embrace the thrilling essence of the character amidst the timeless contrast of black and white."

After creating the design, I decided to edit the levels in GIMP in greyscale image mode to give it that extra touch of depth and detail. The whole process only took me a day, and I'm really happy with the results.

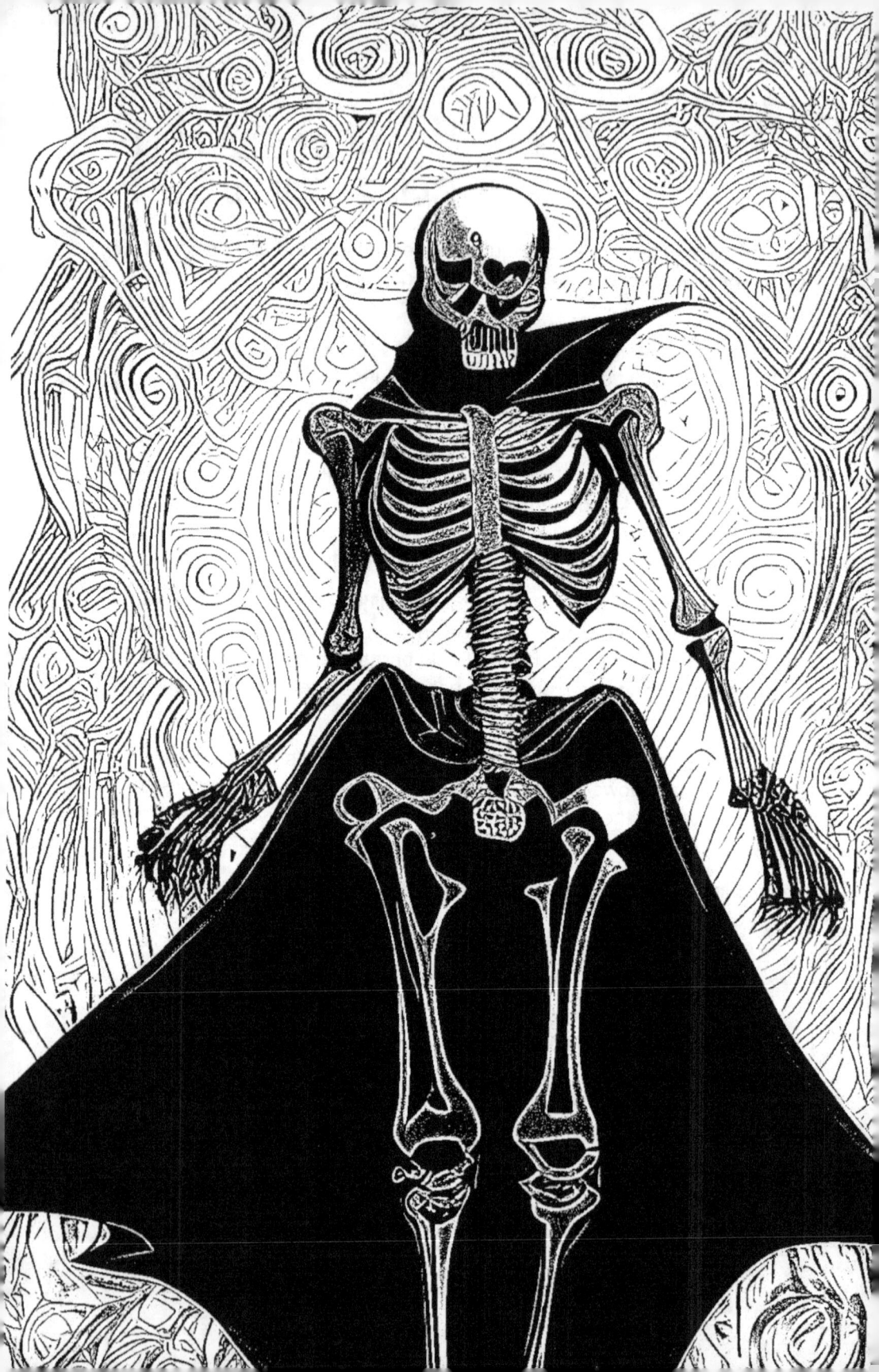

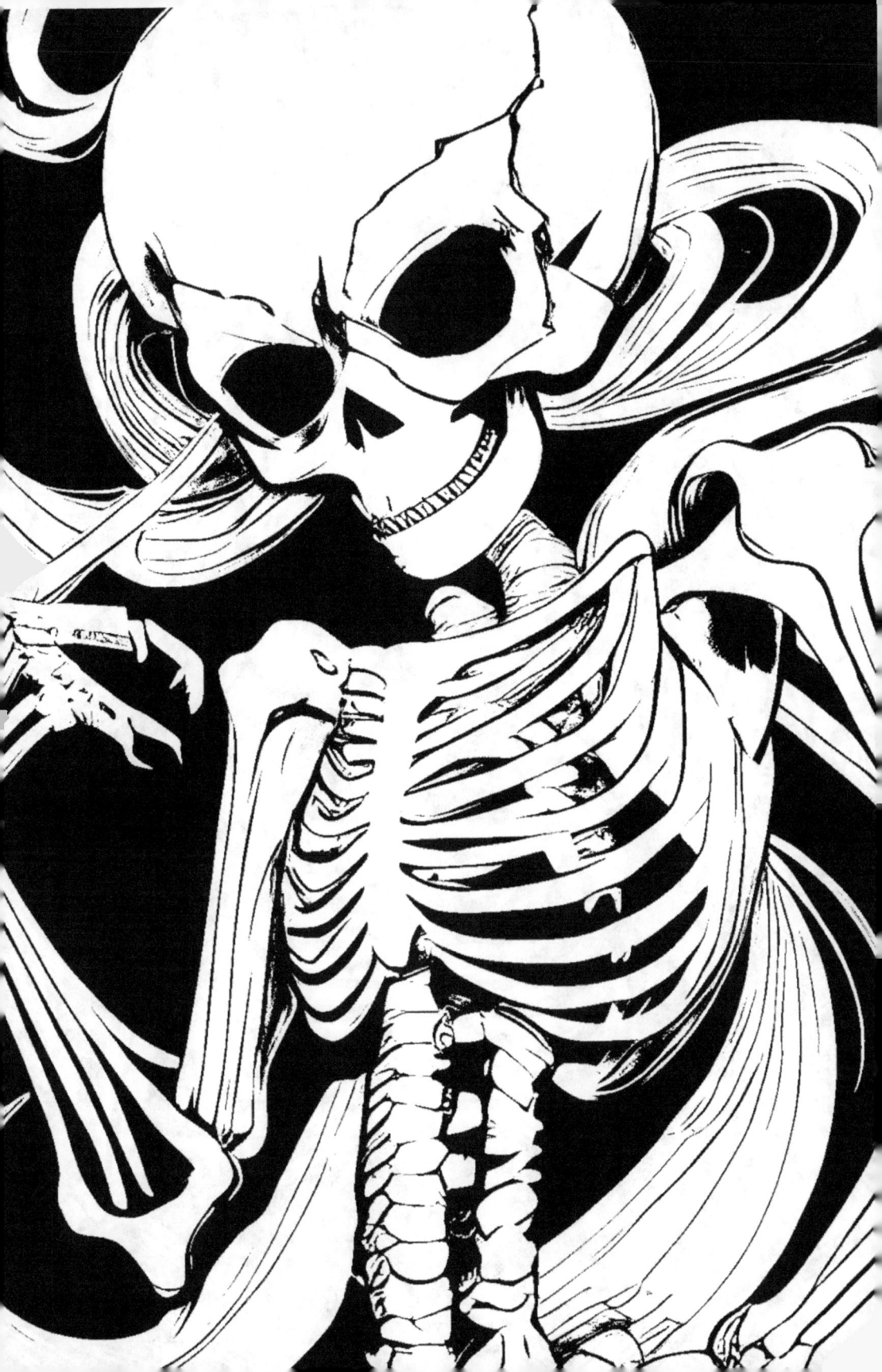

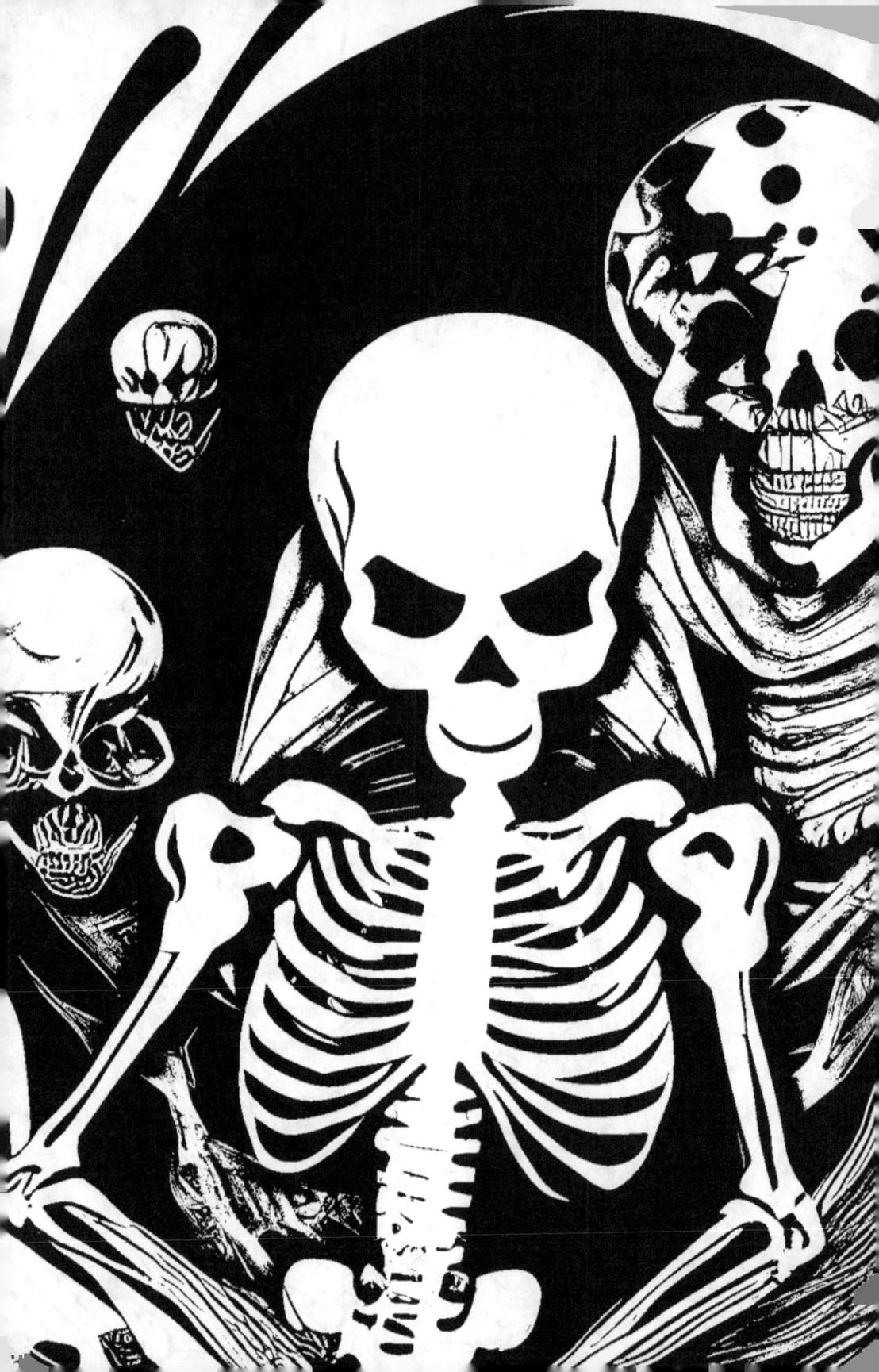

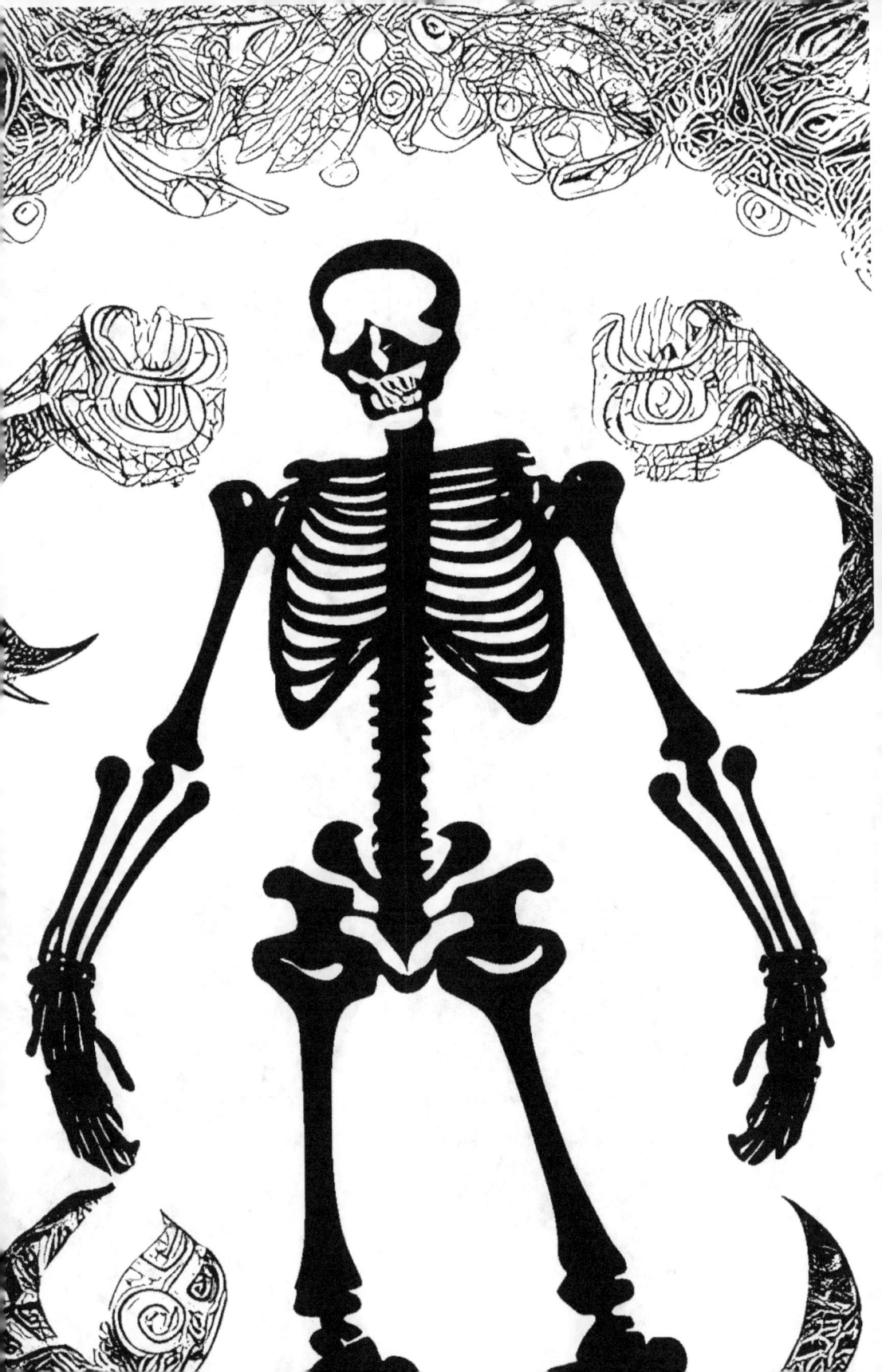

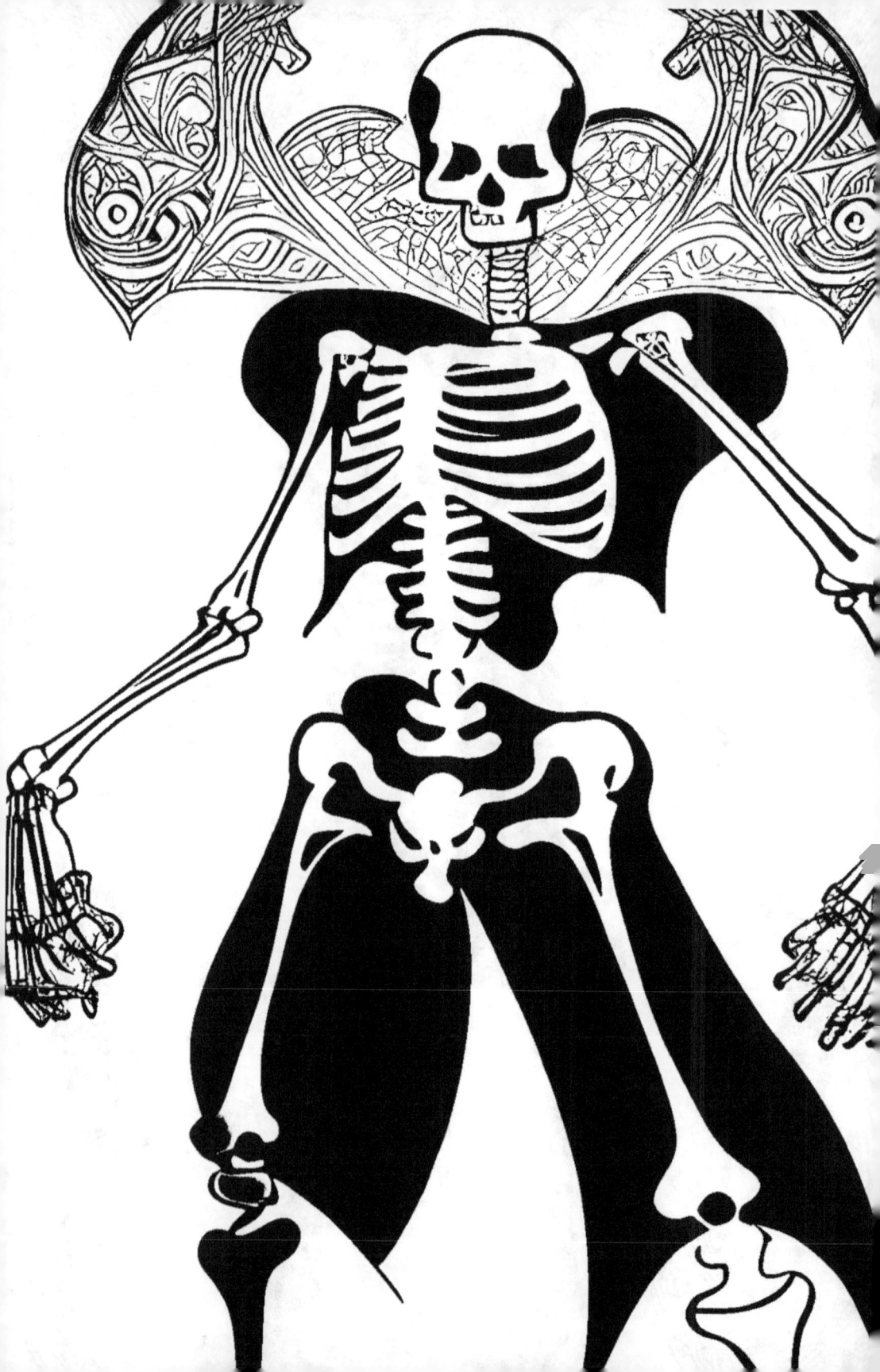

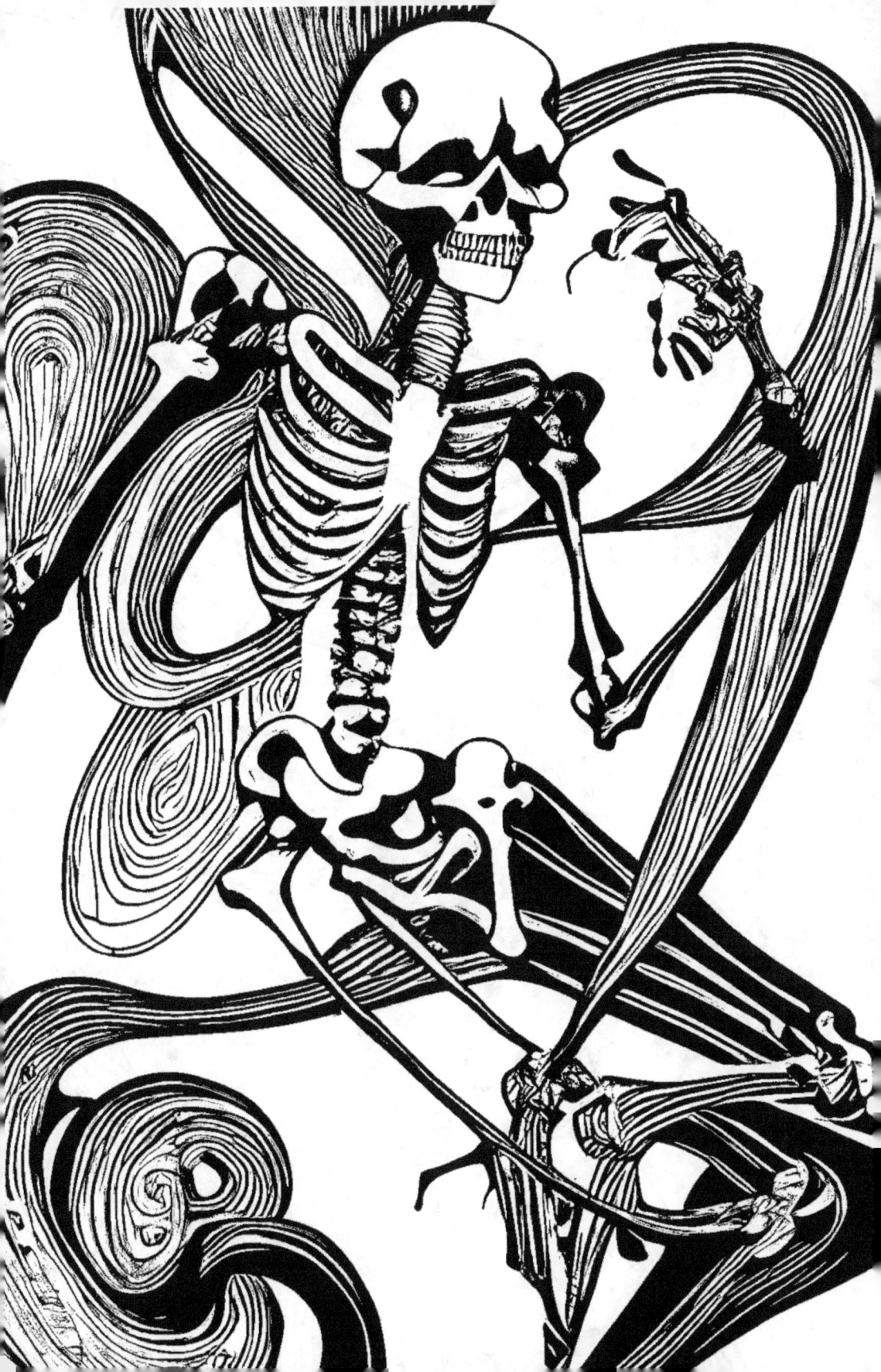

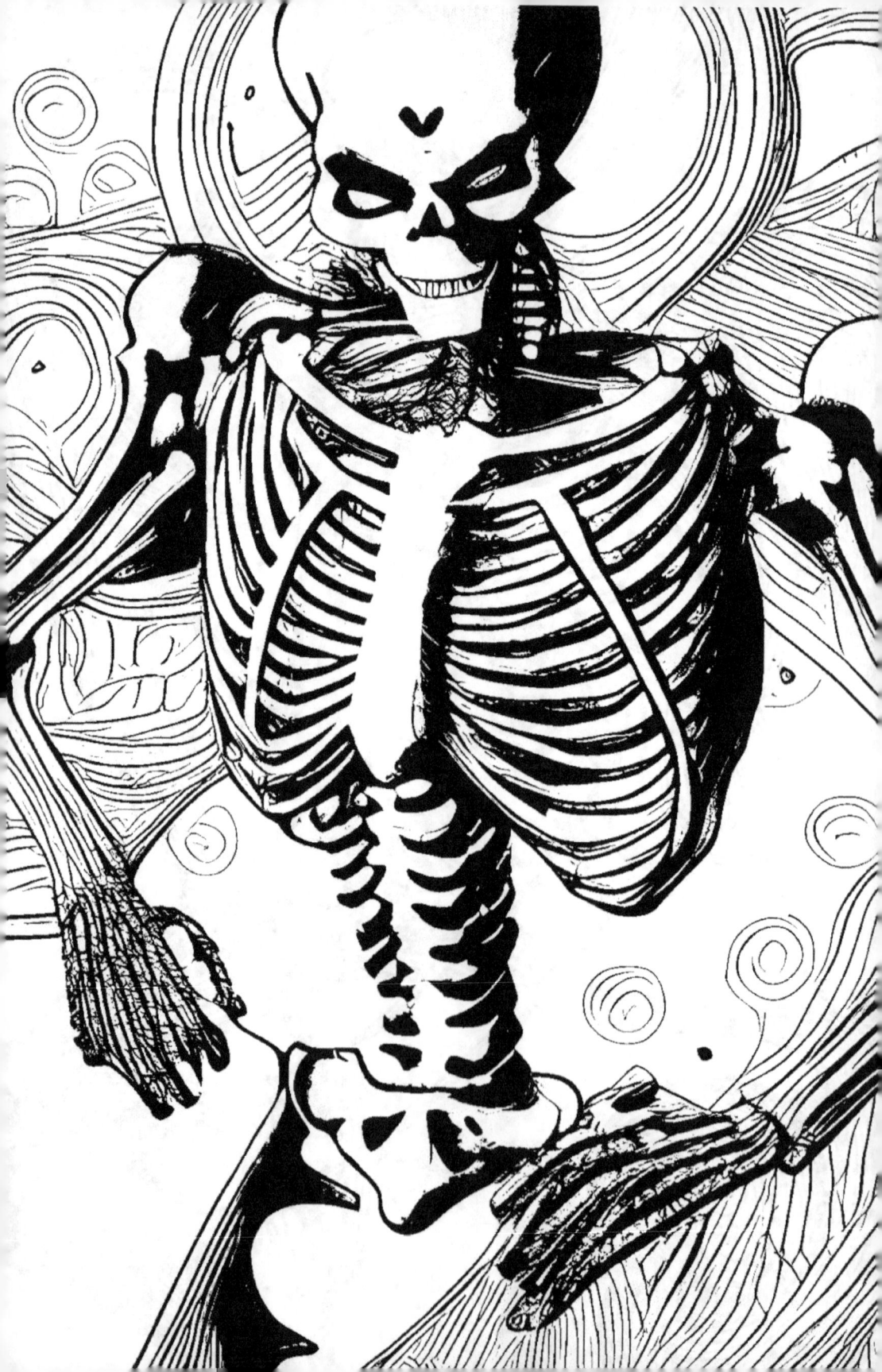

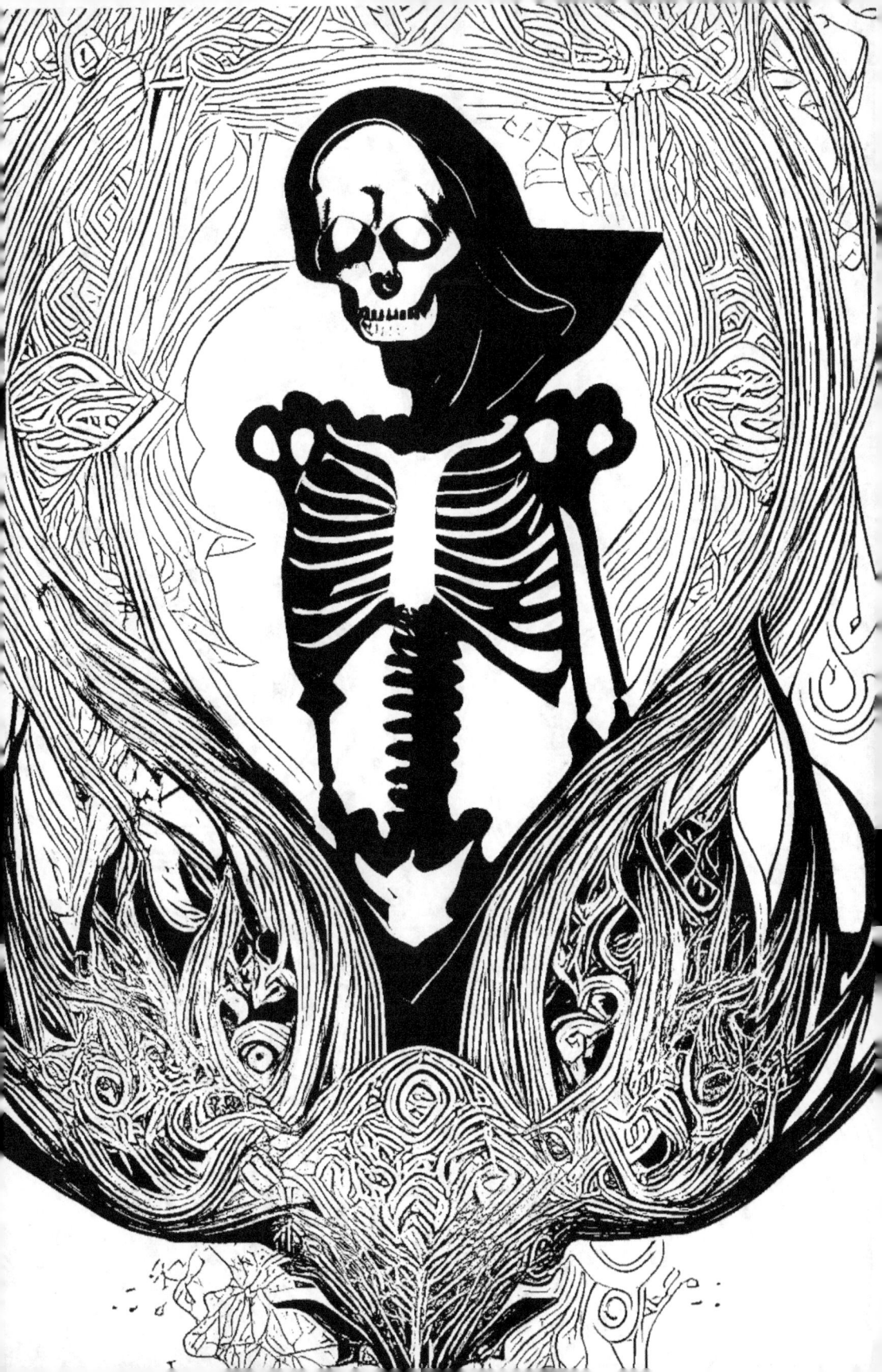

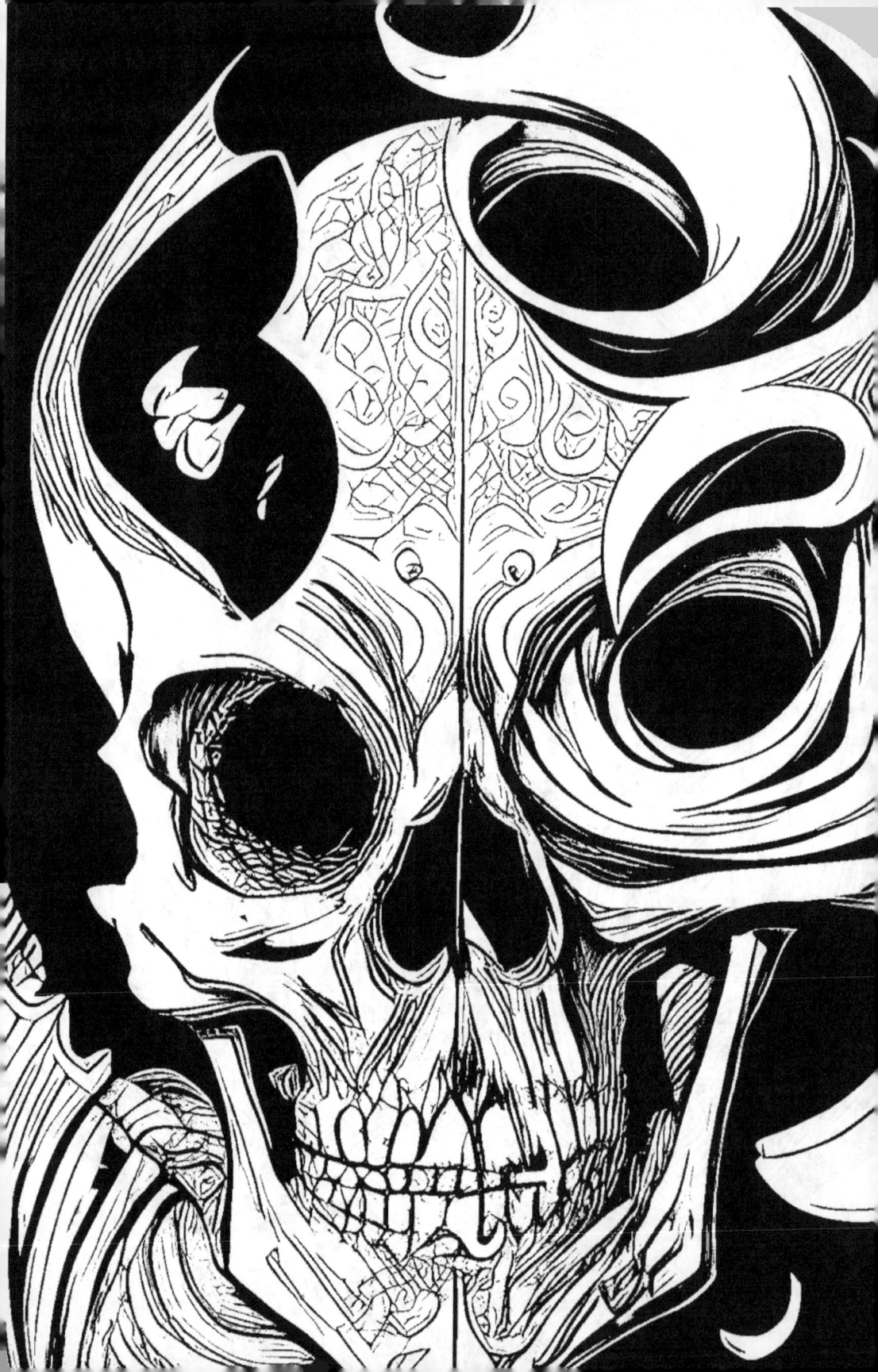

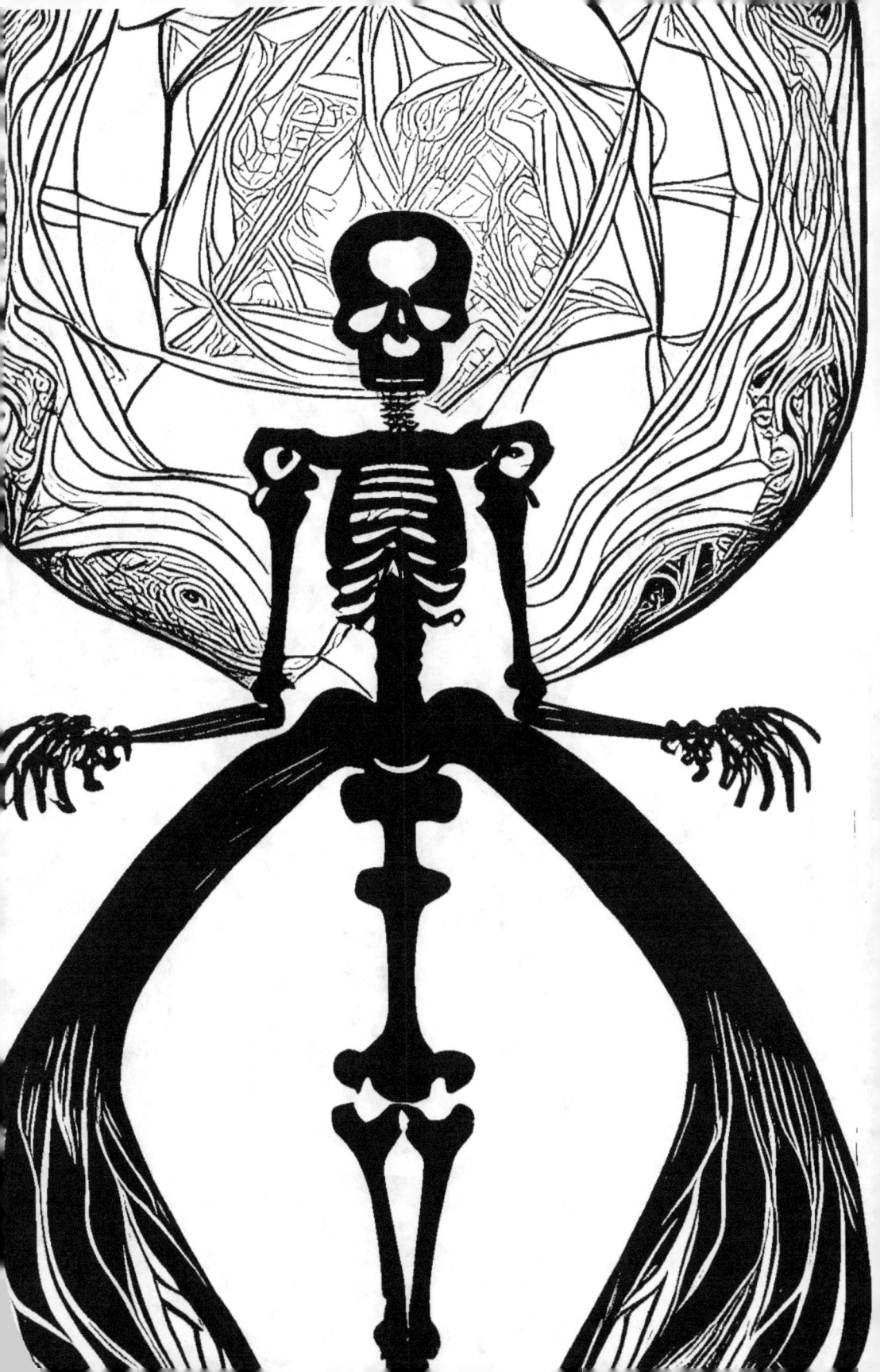

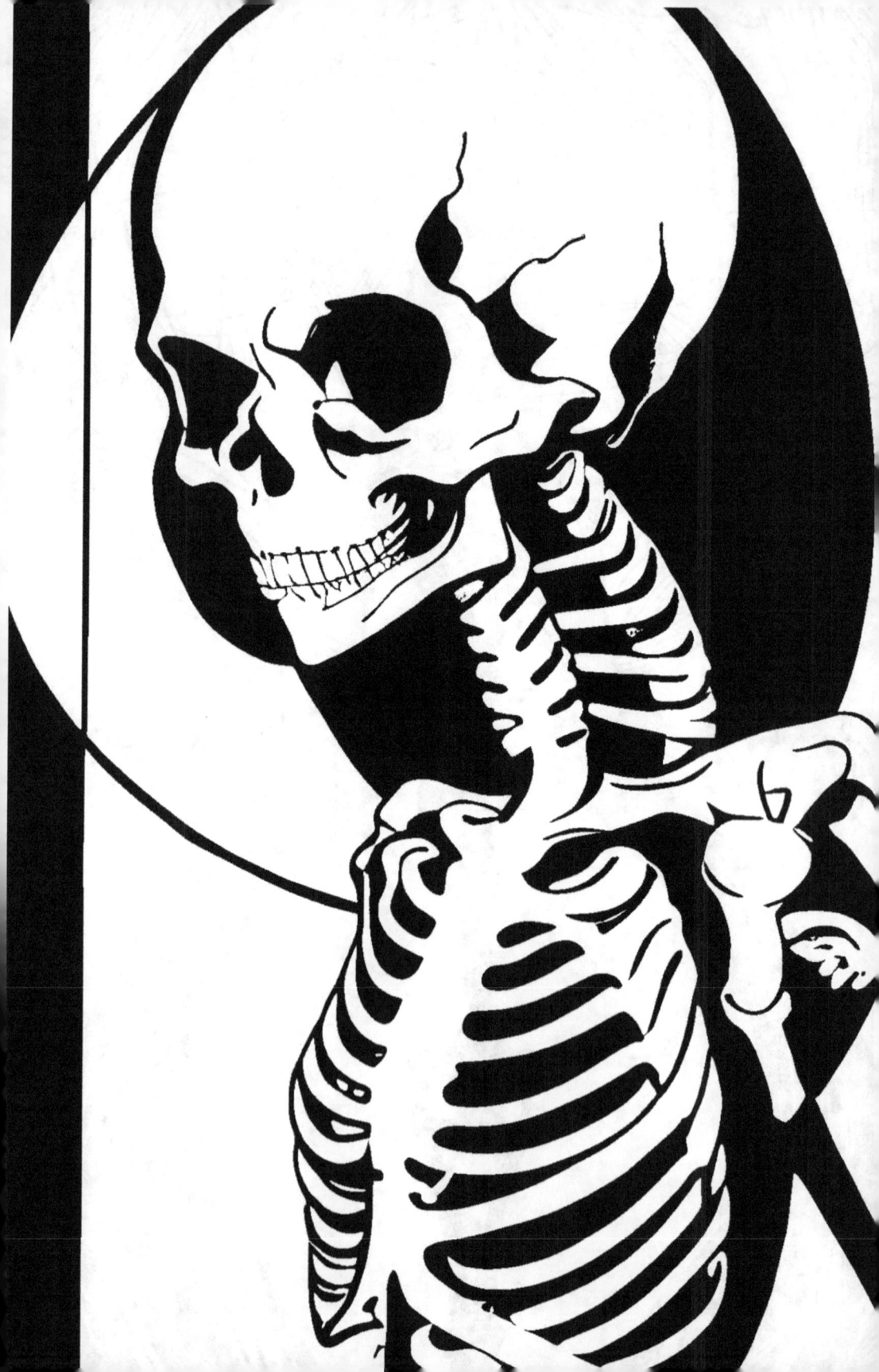

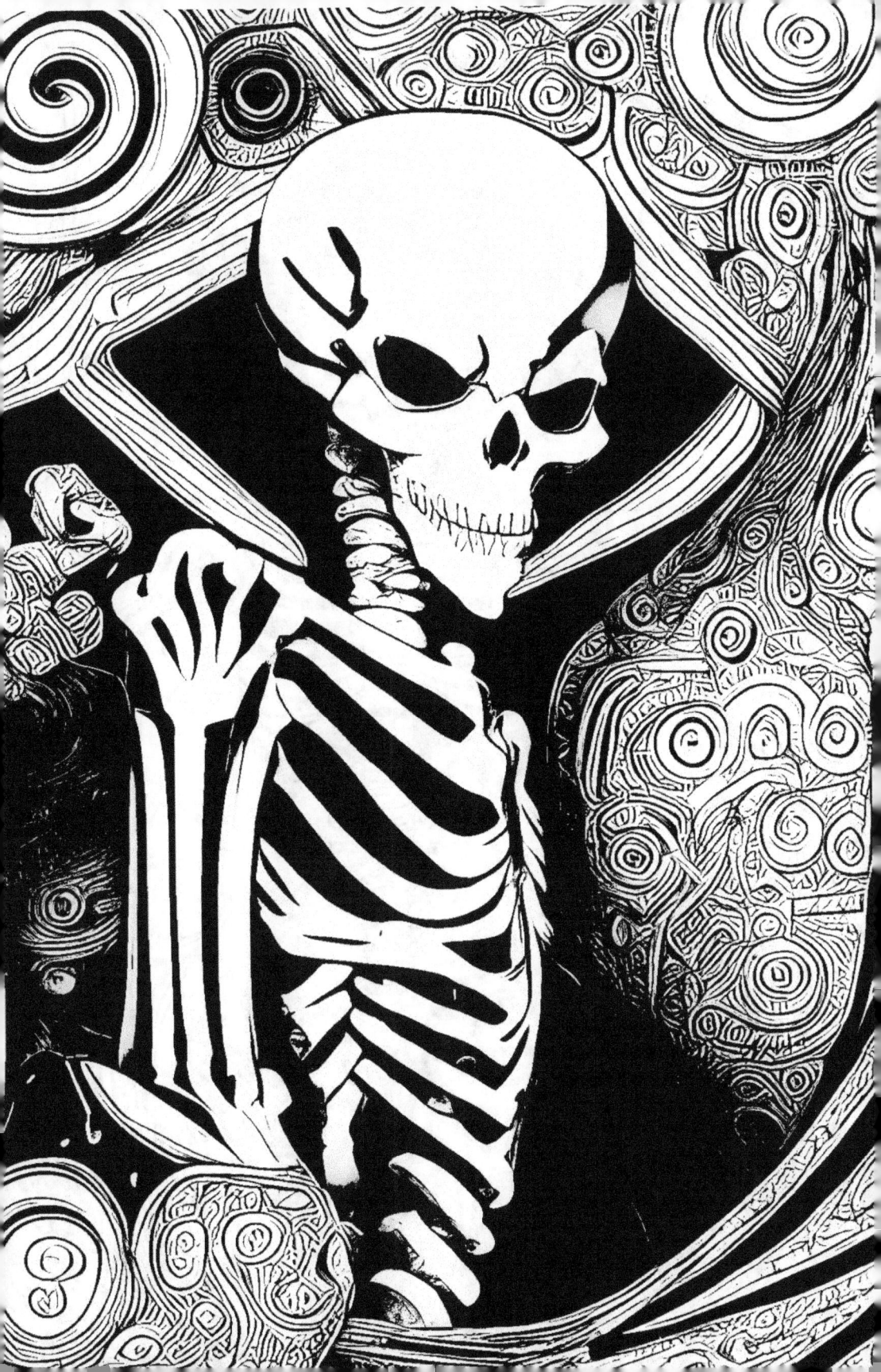

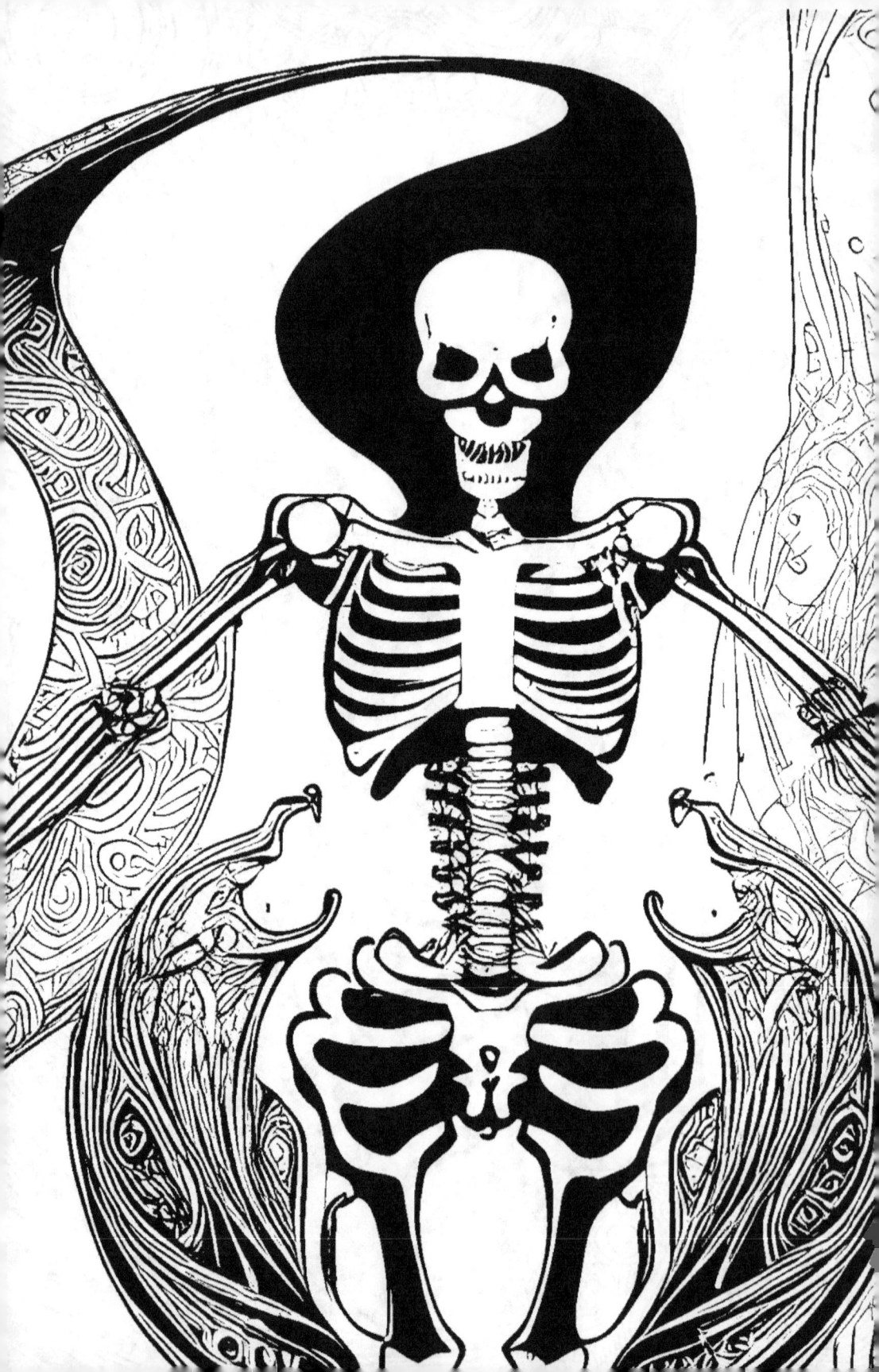

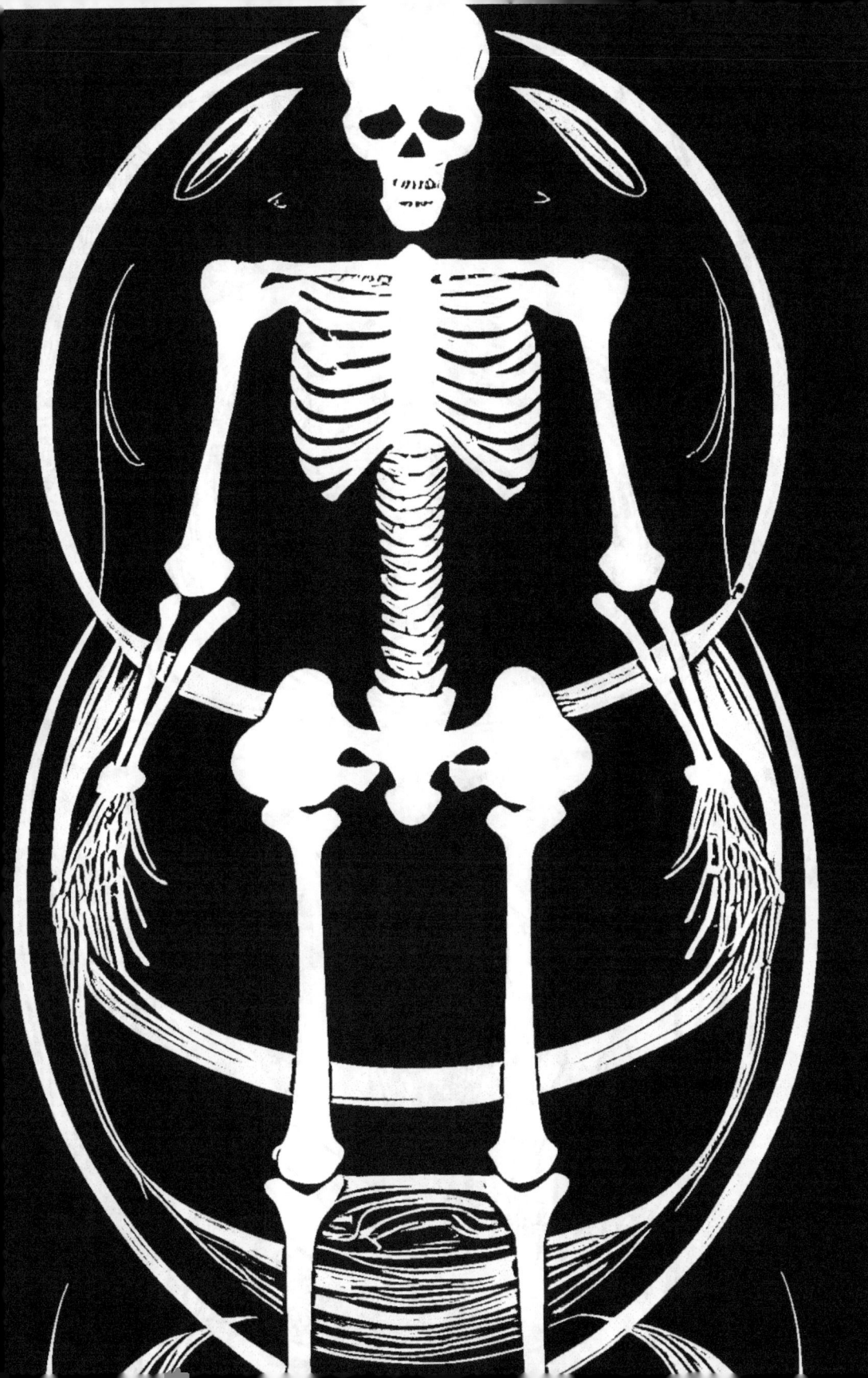

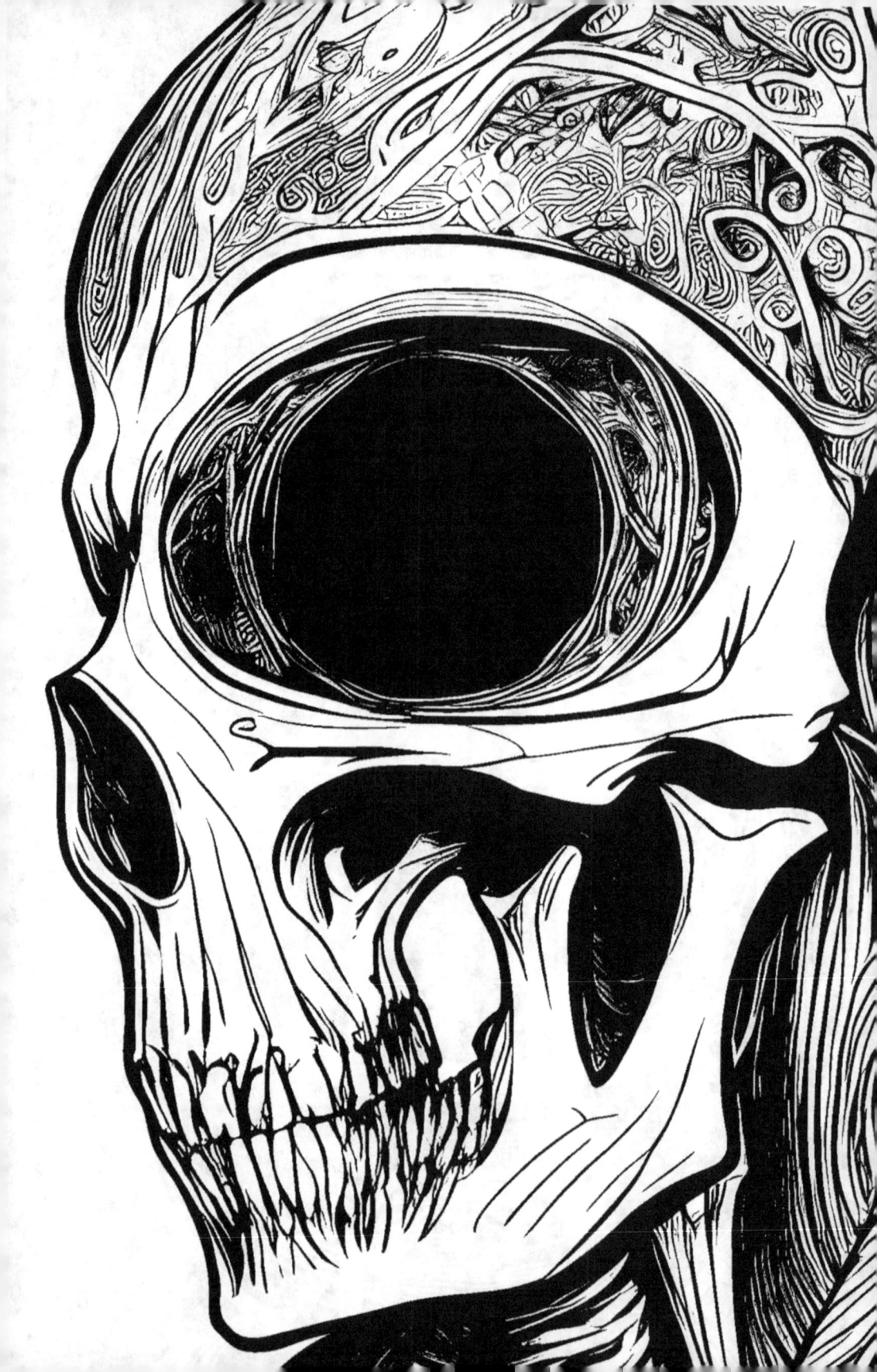

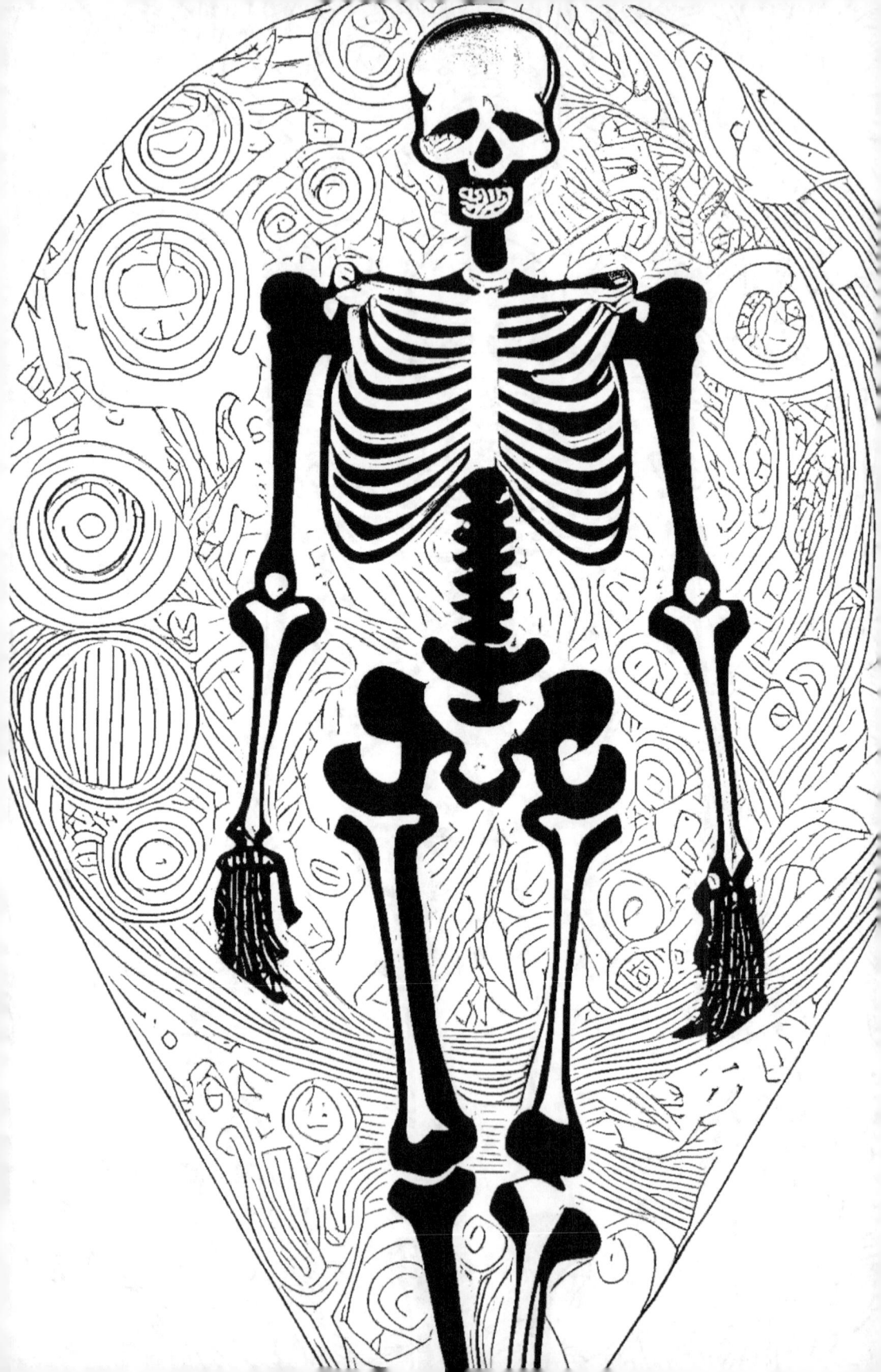

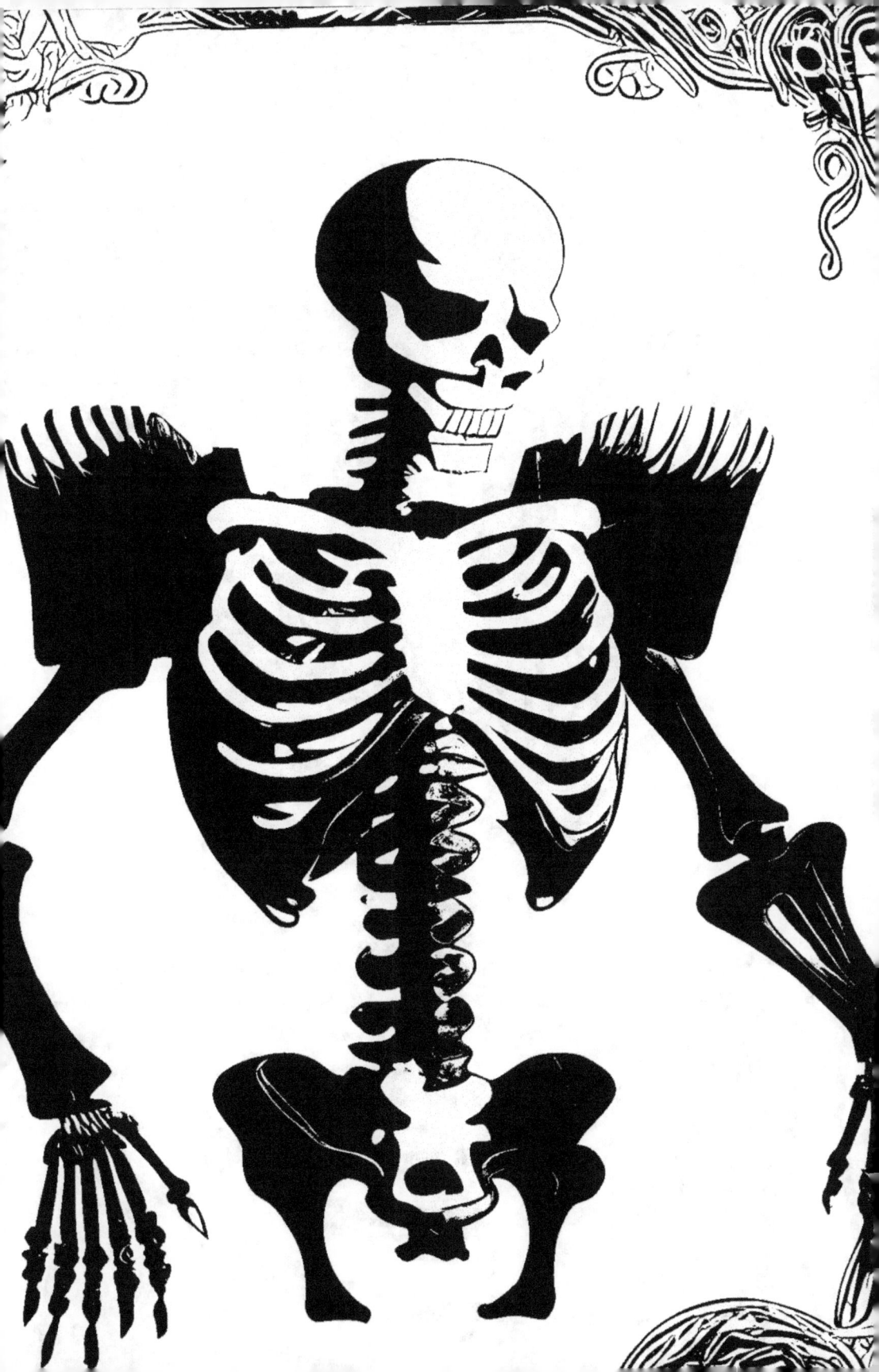

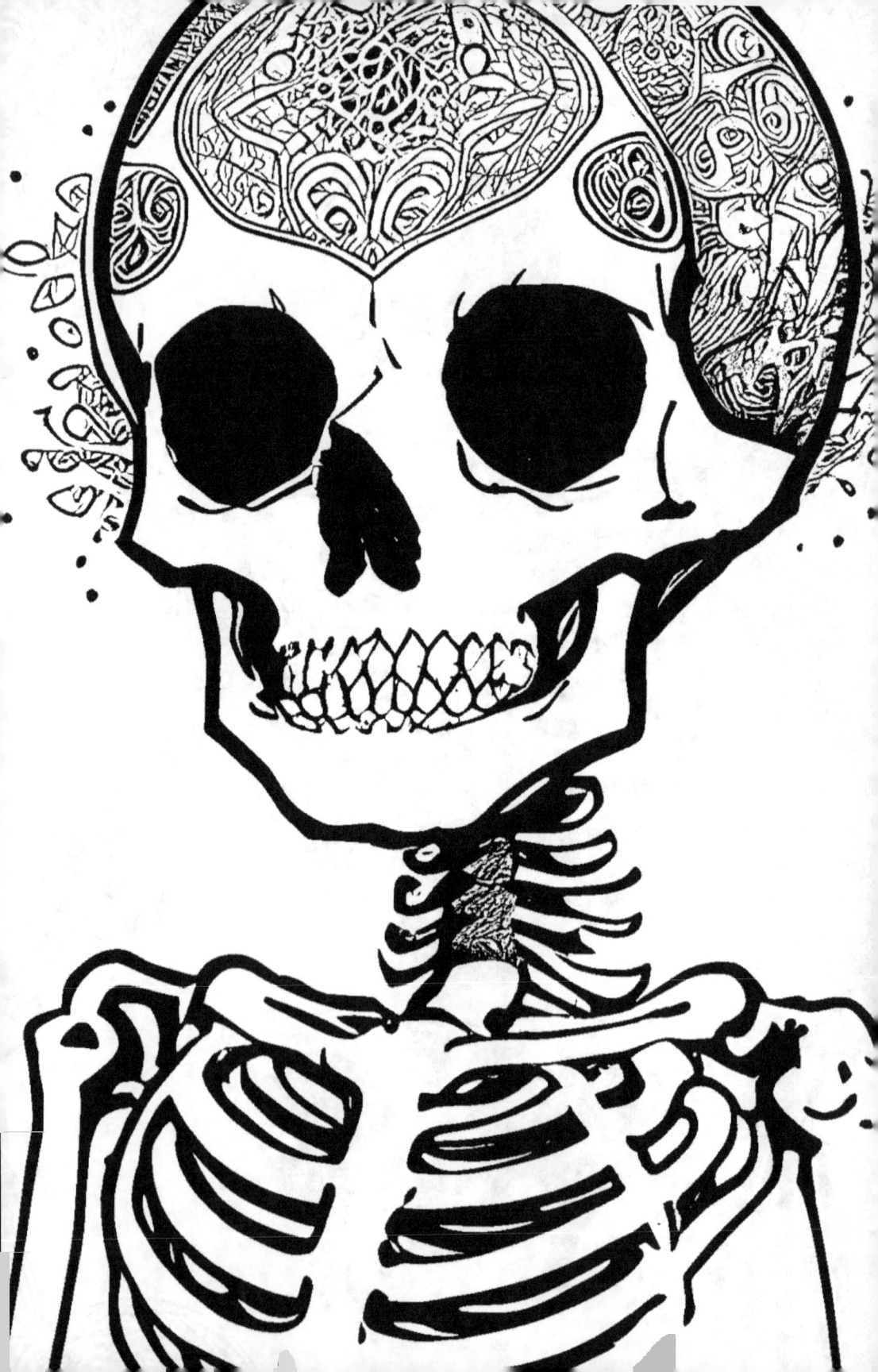

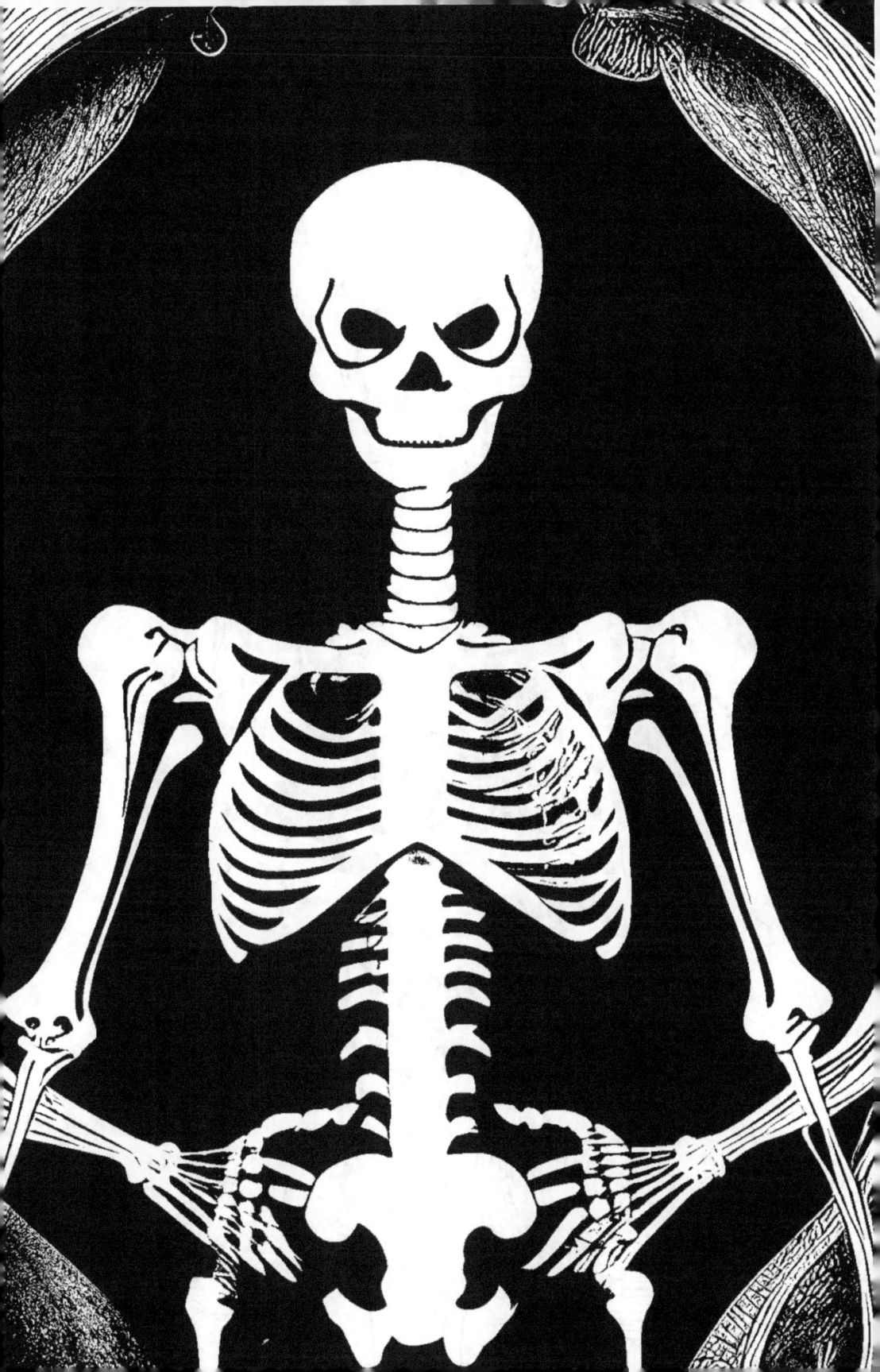

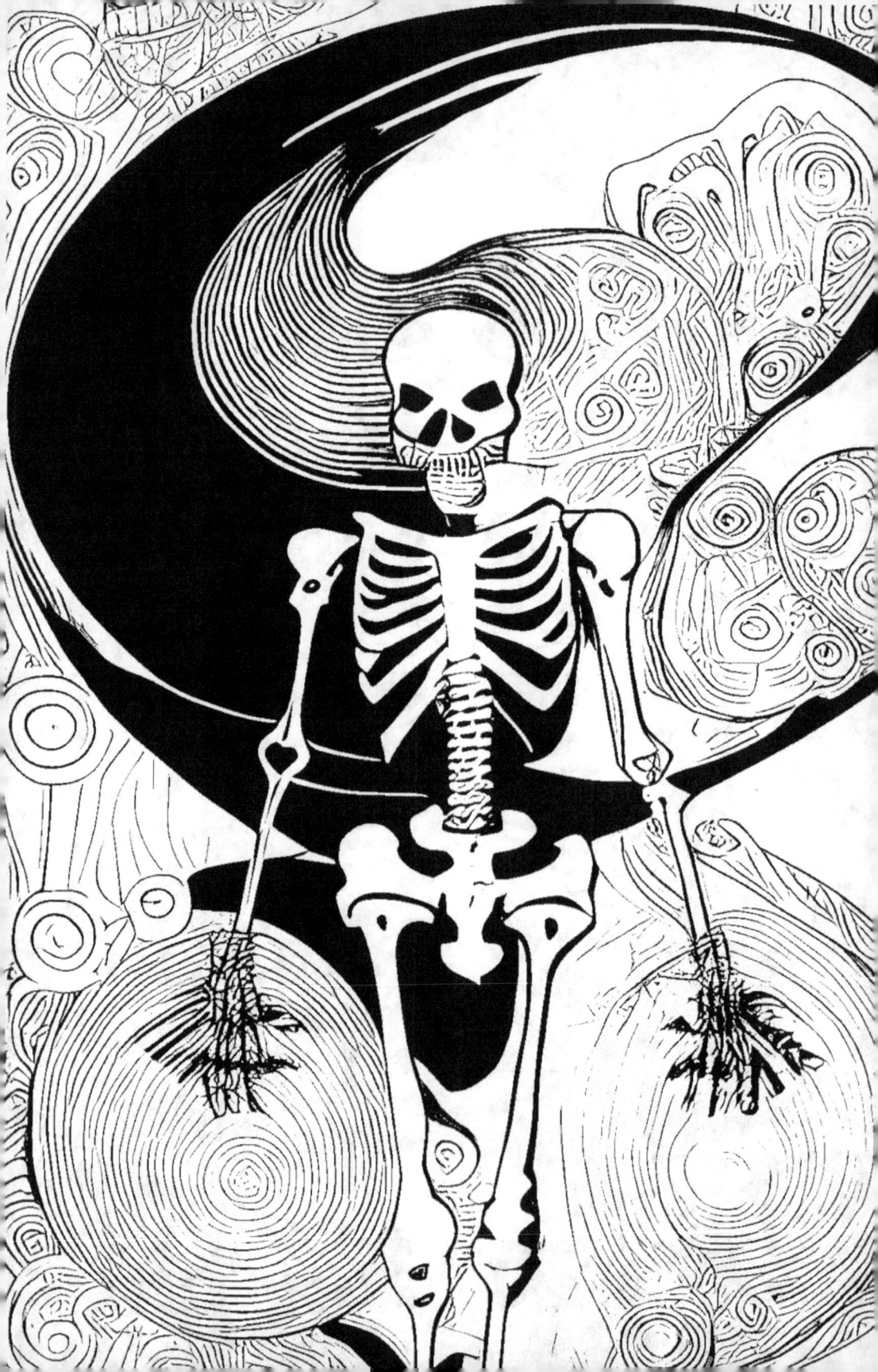

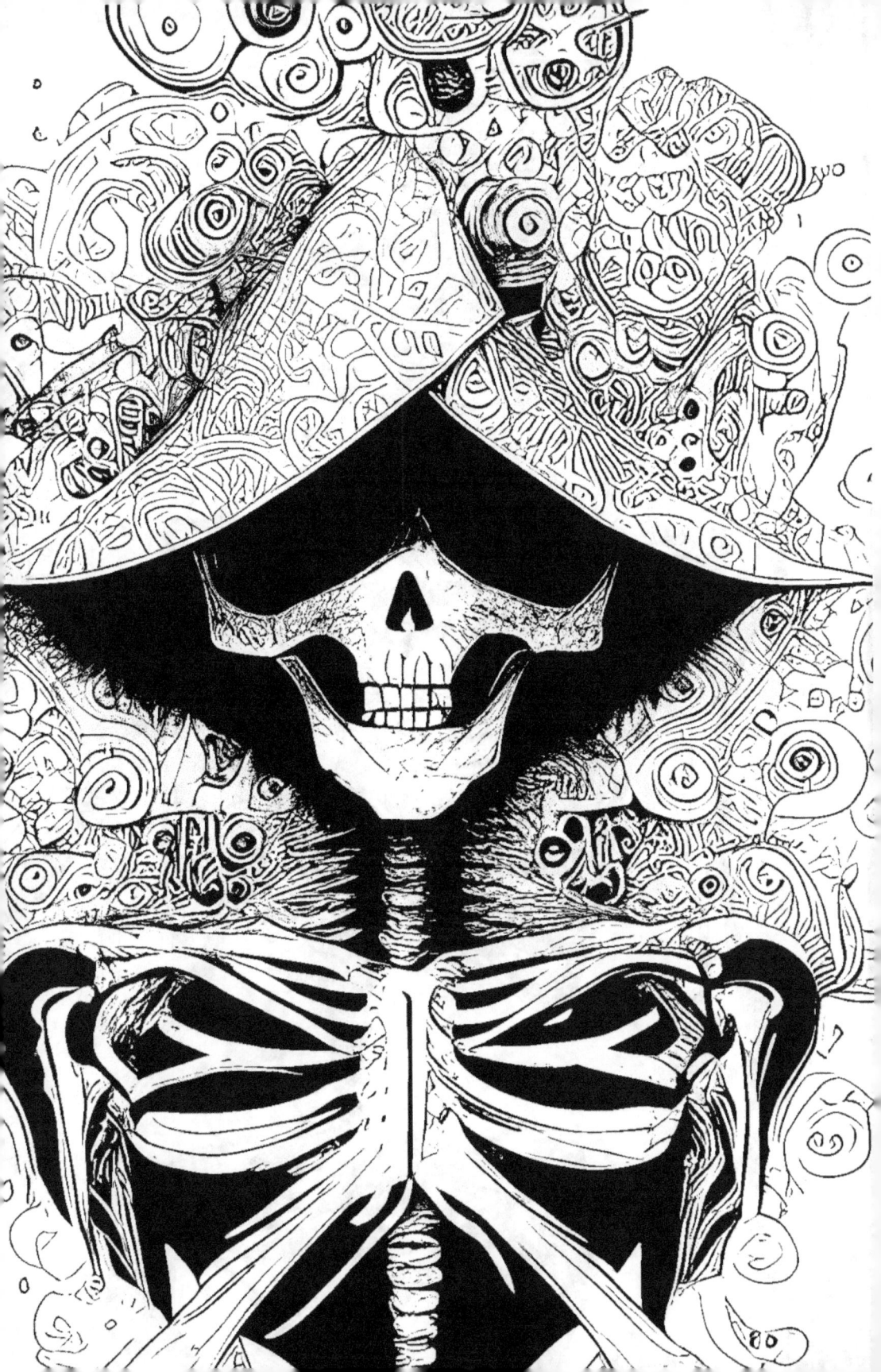

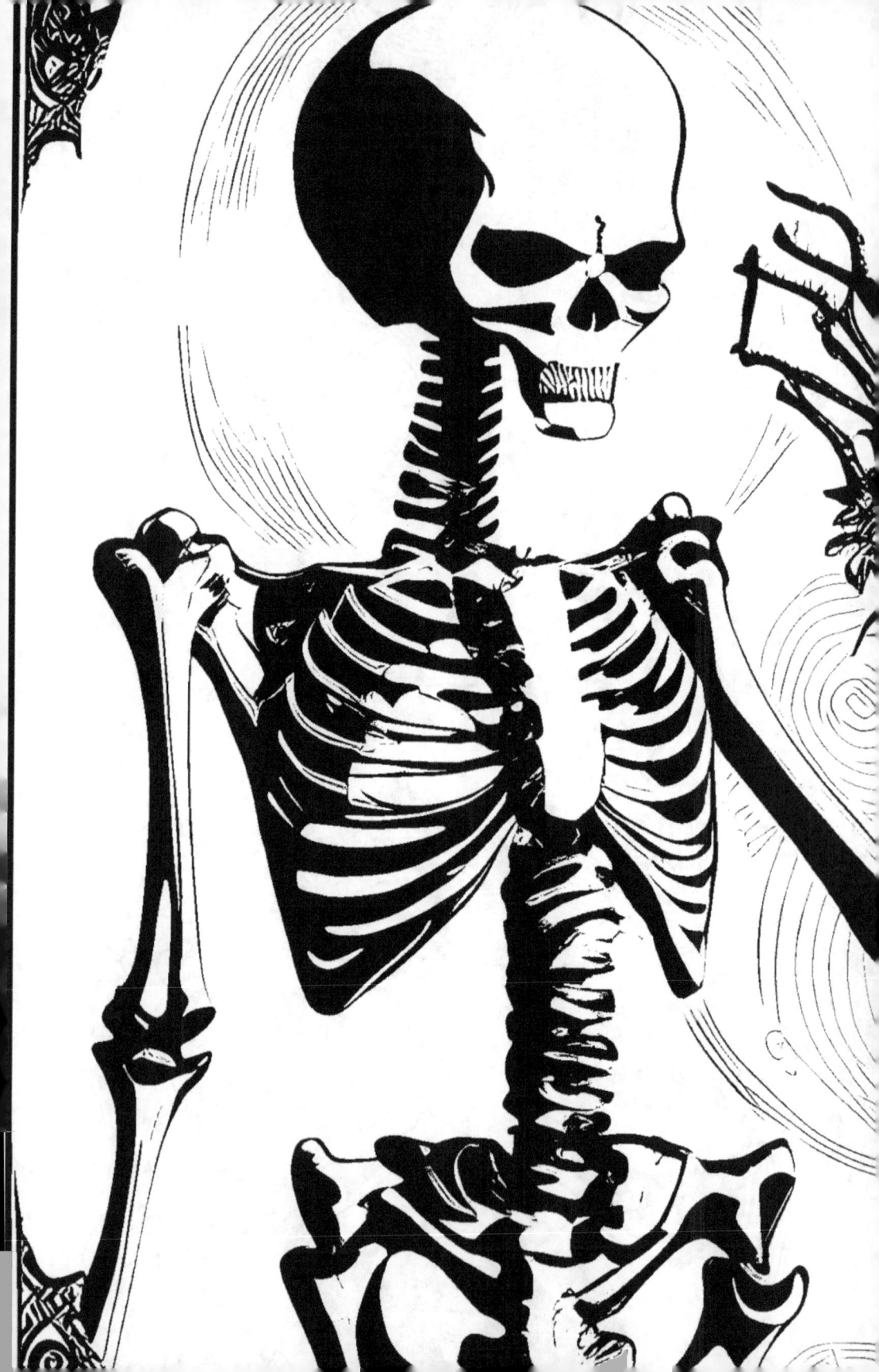

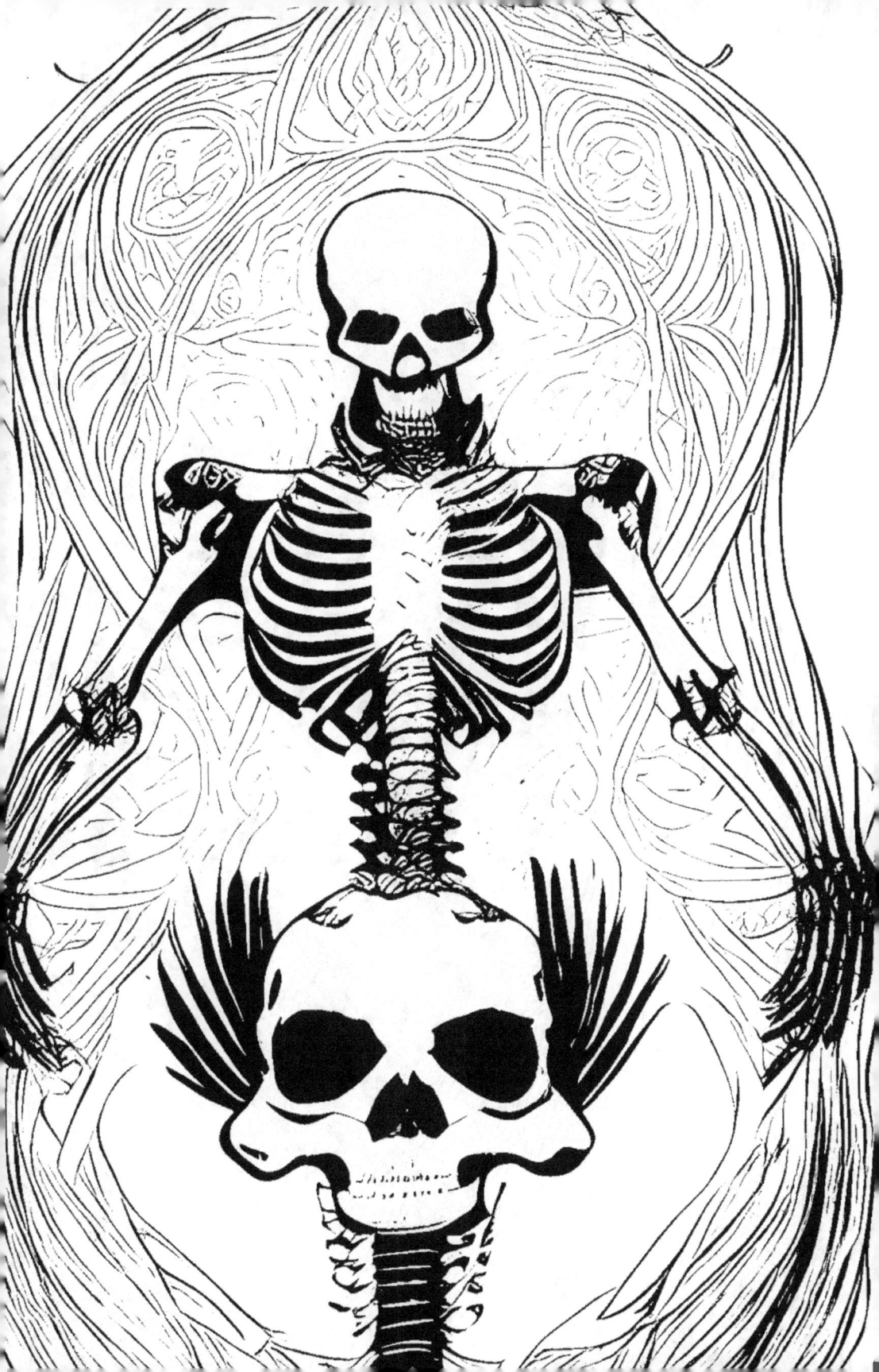

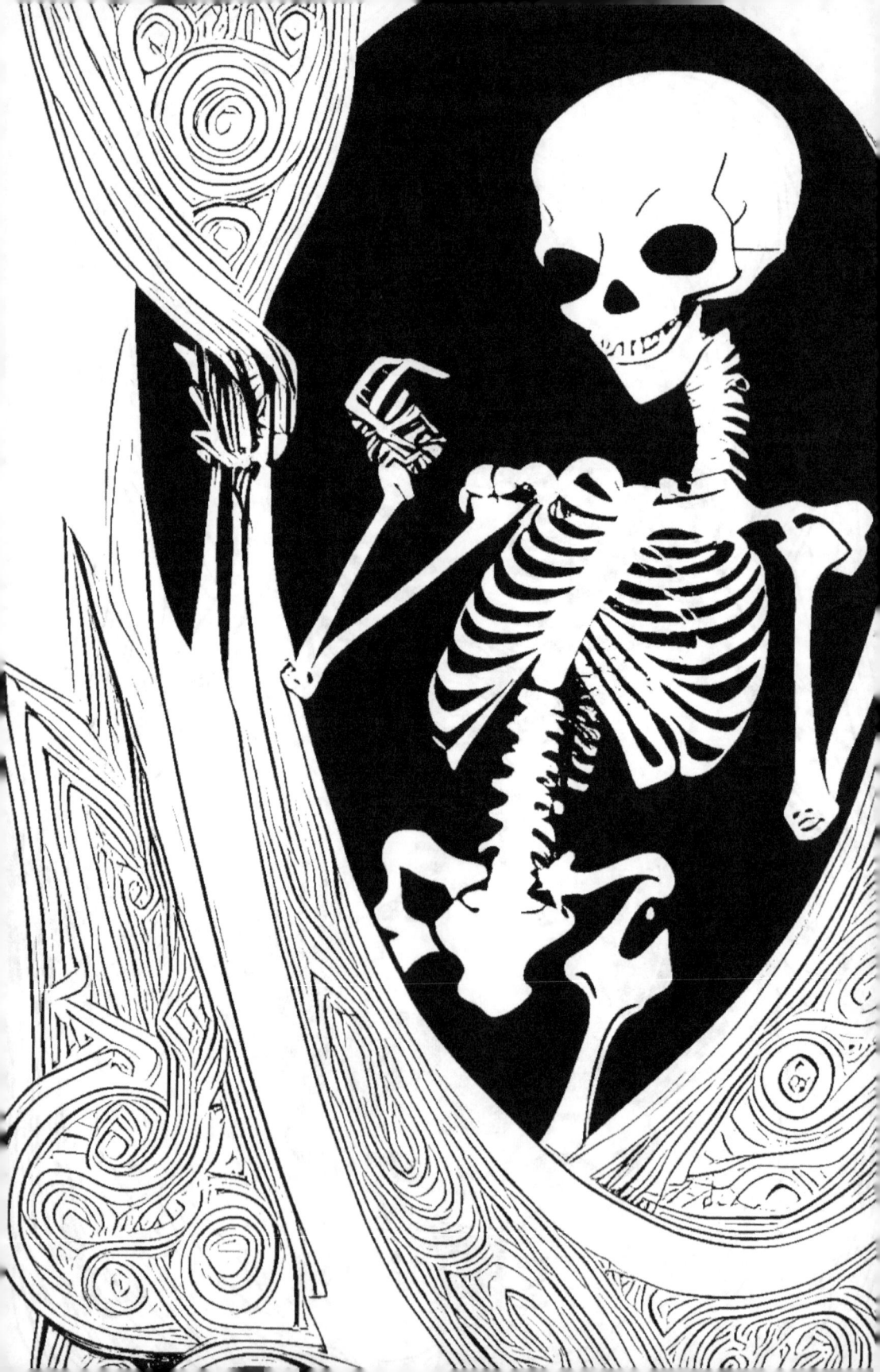

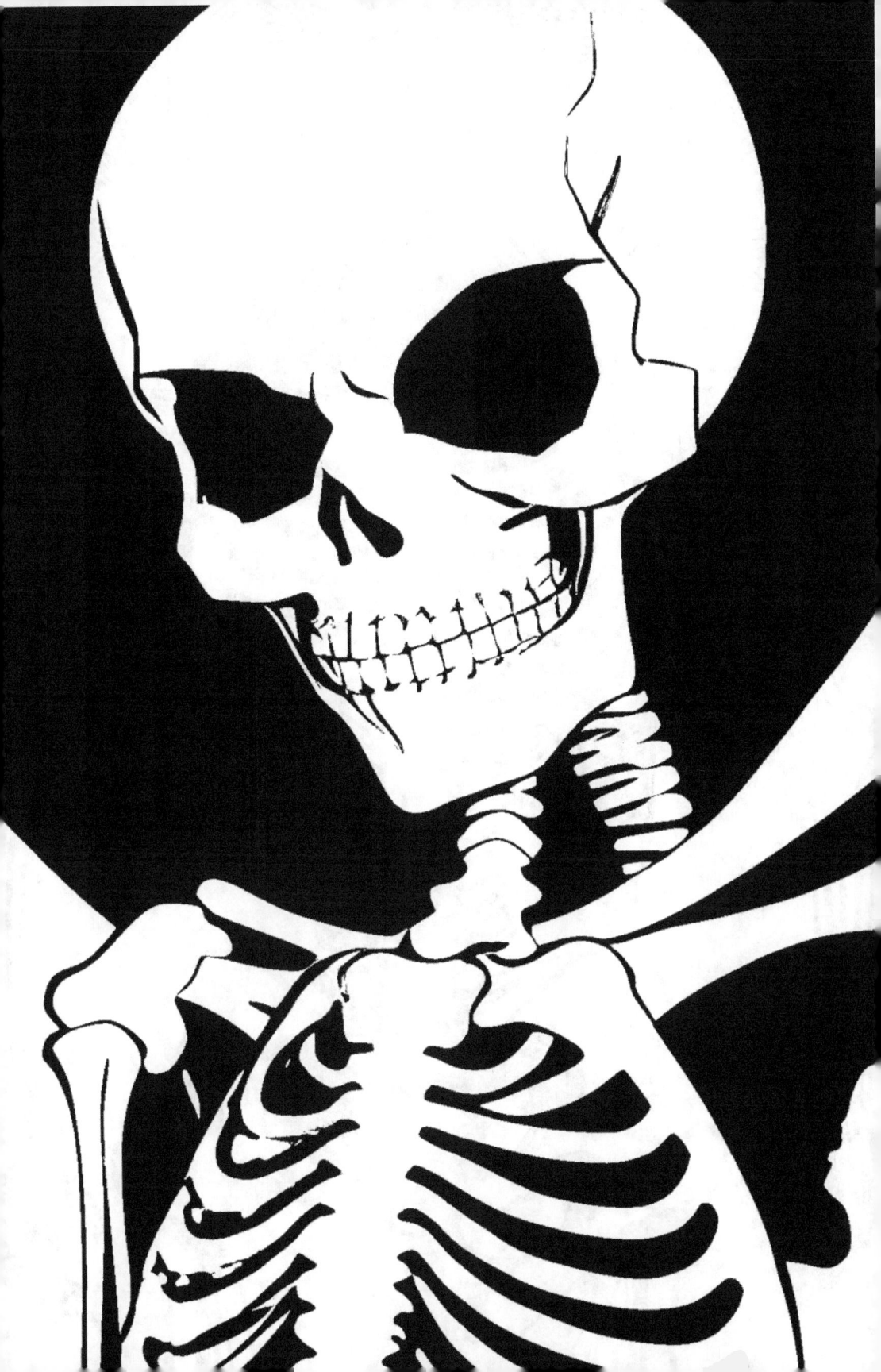

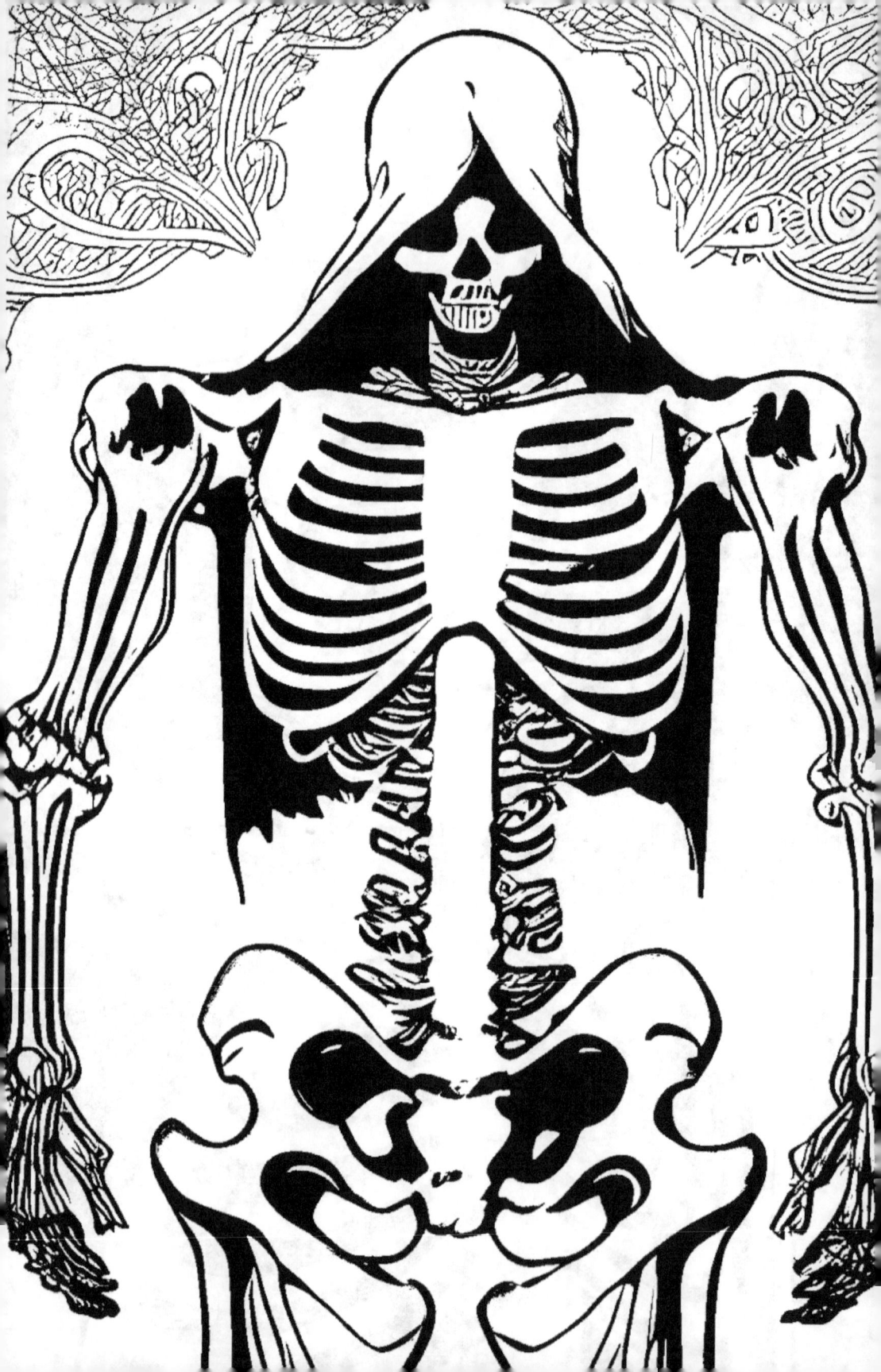

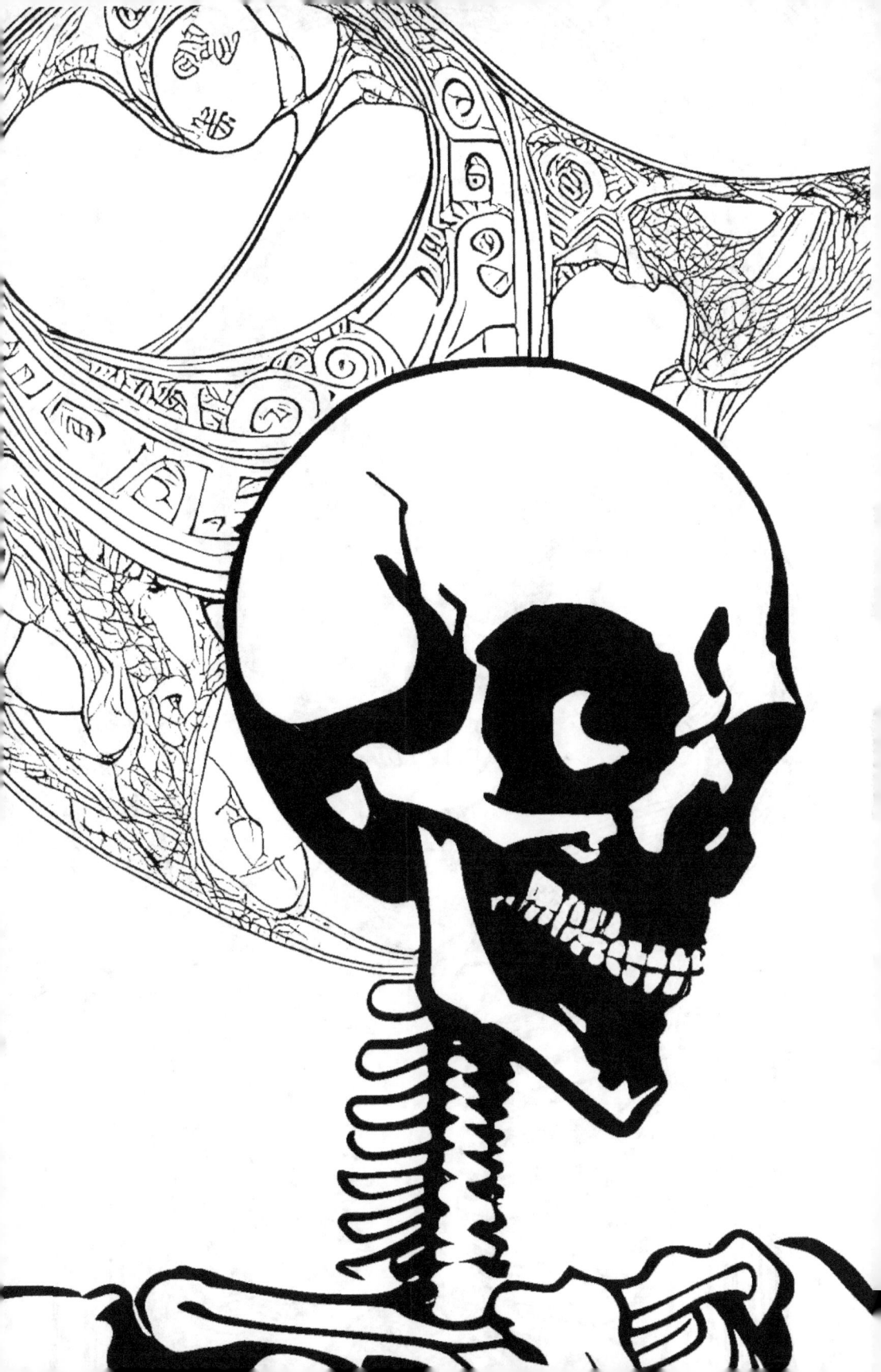

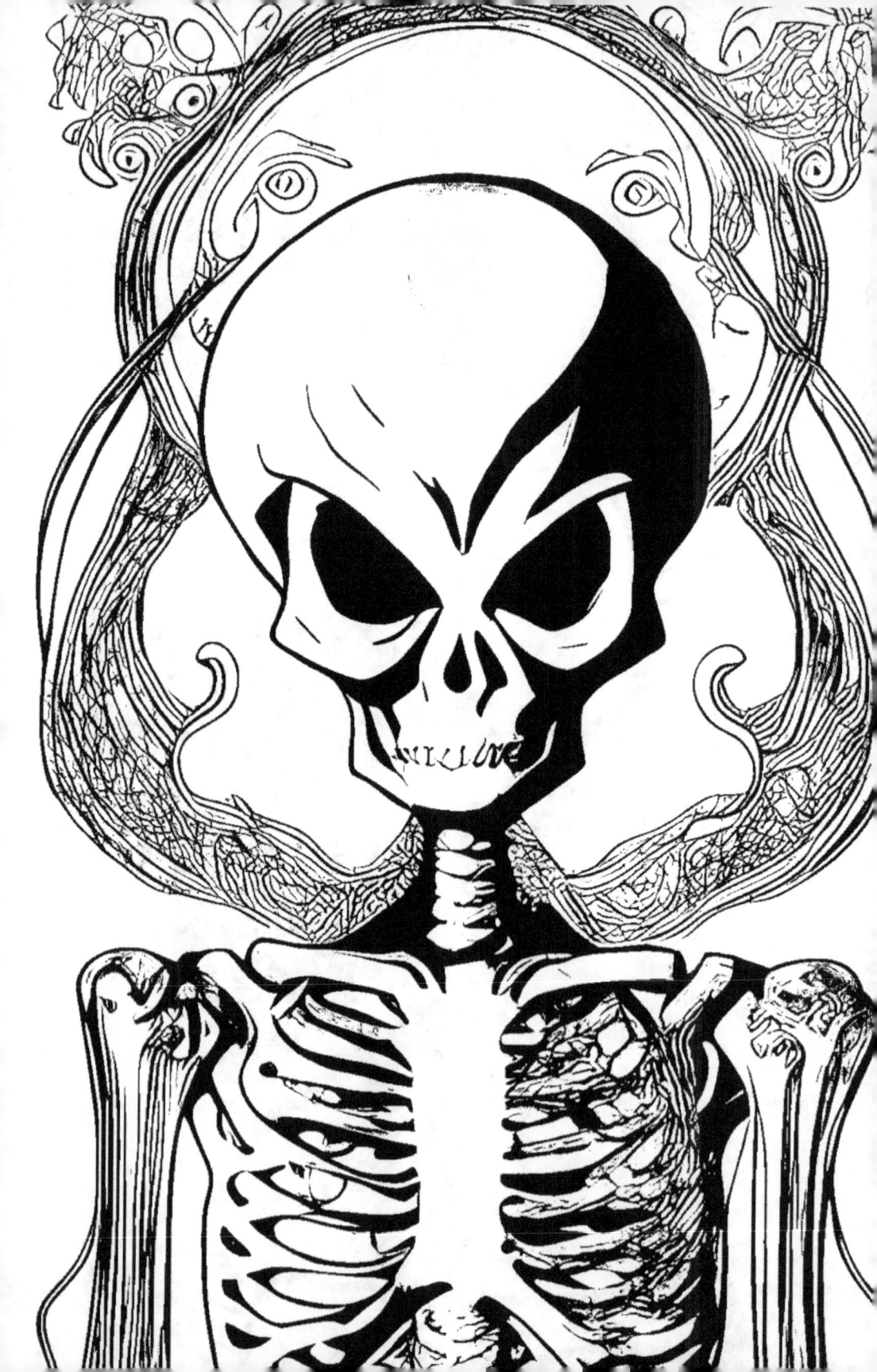

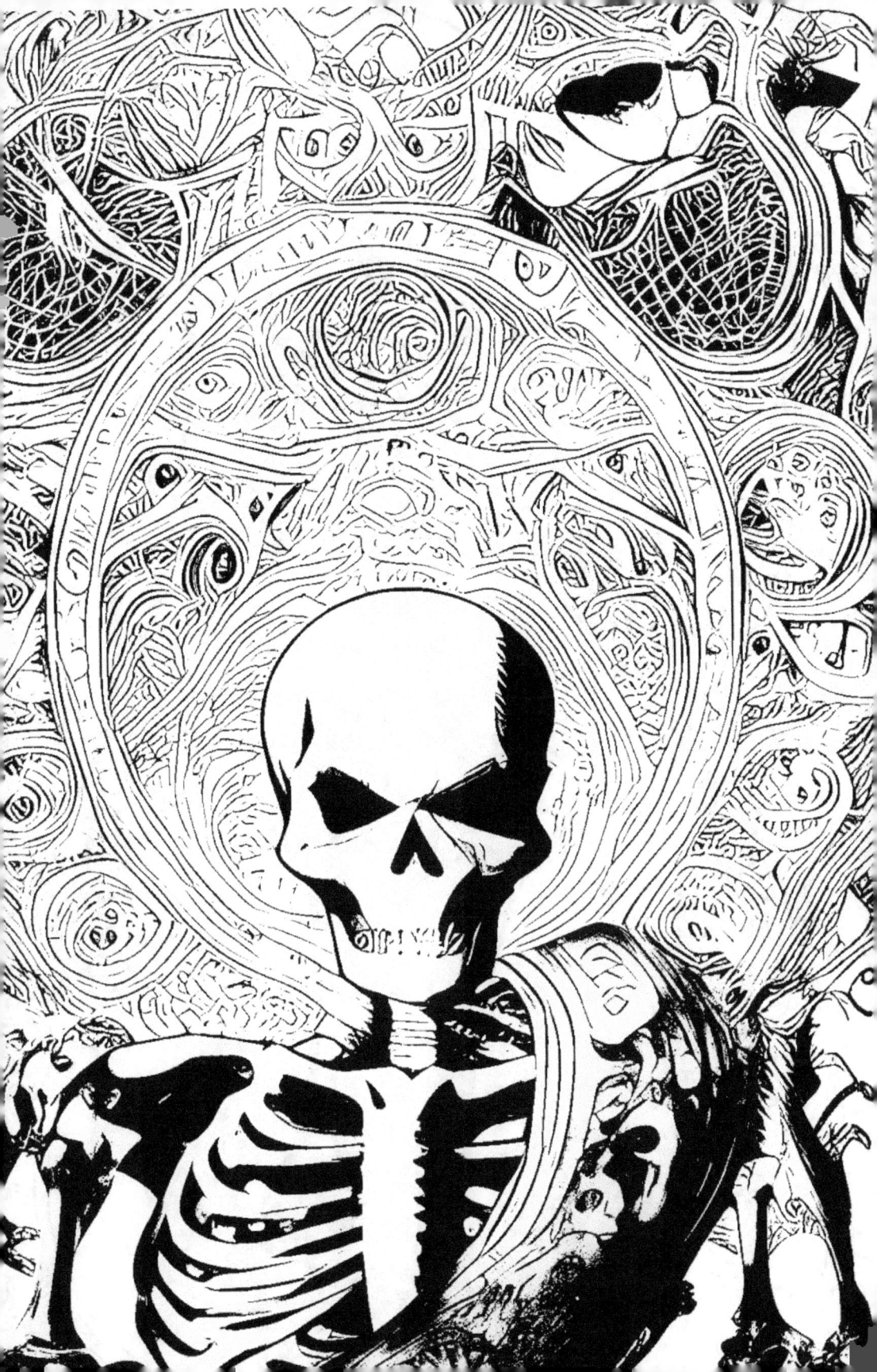

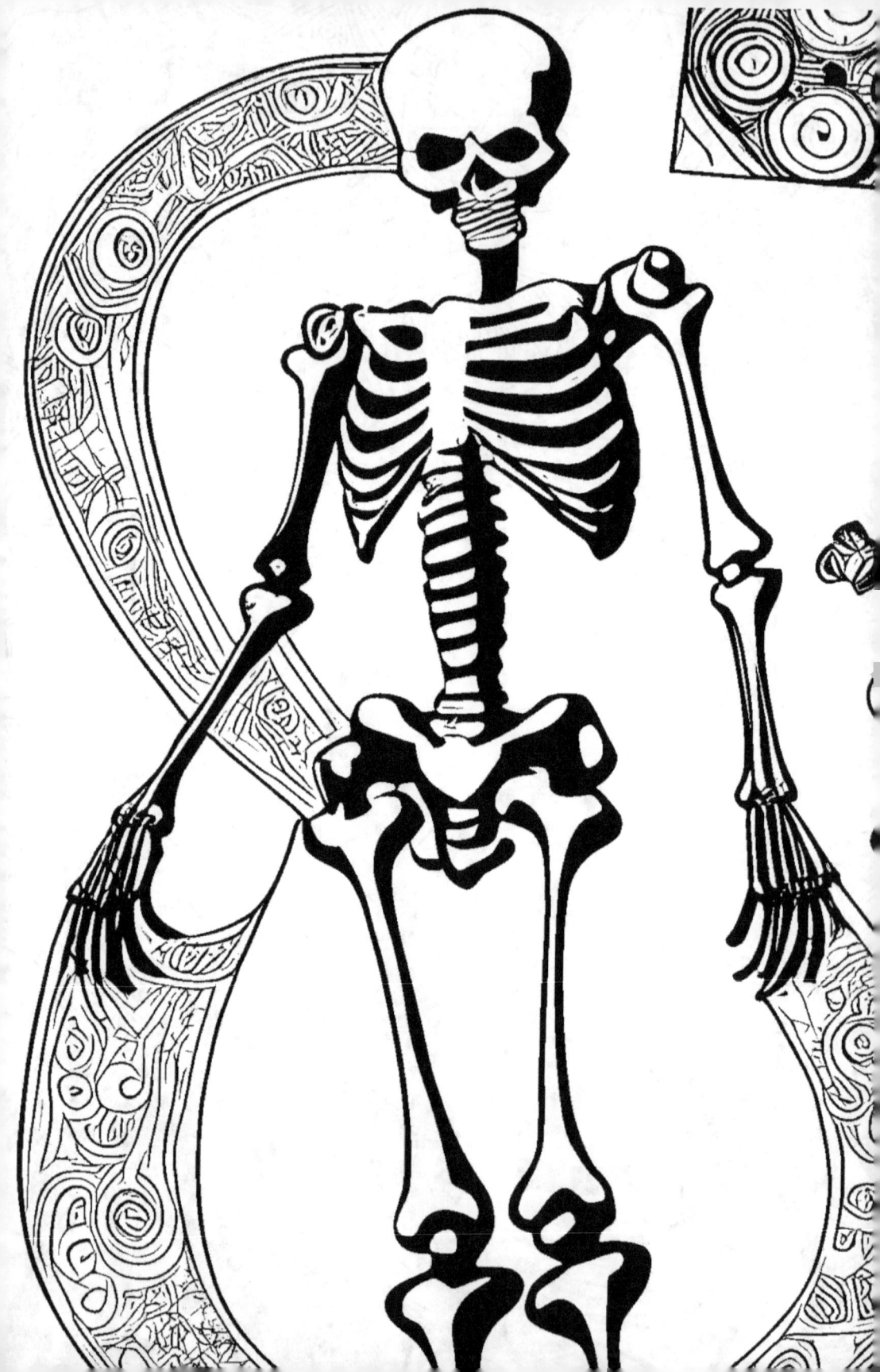

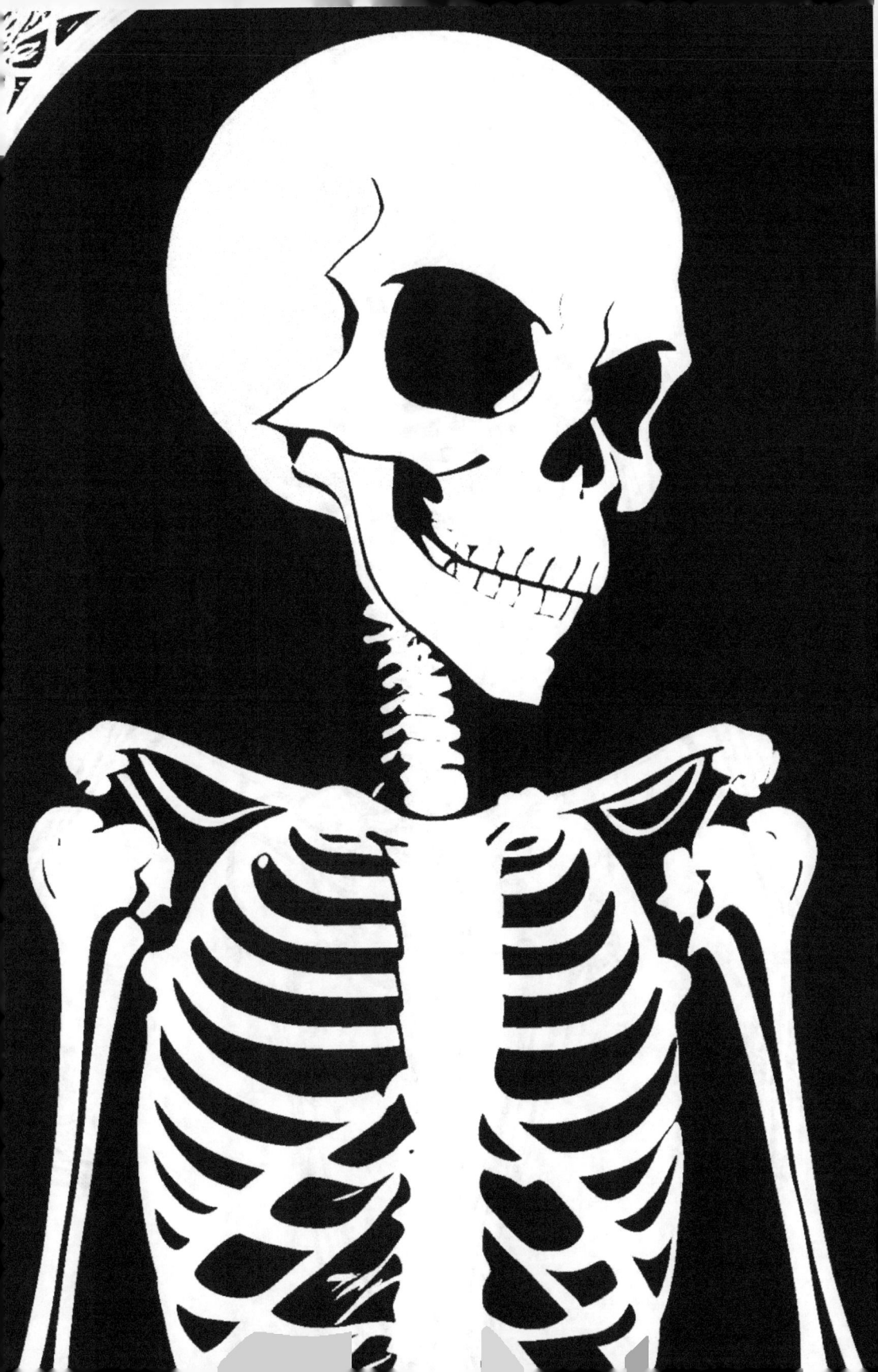

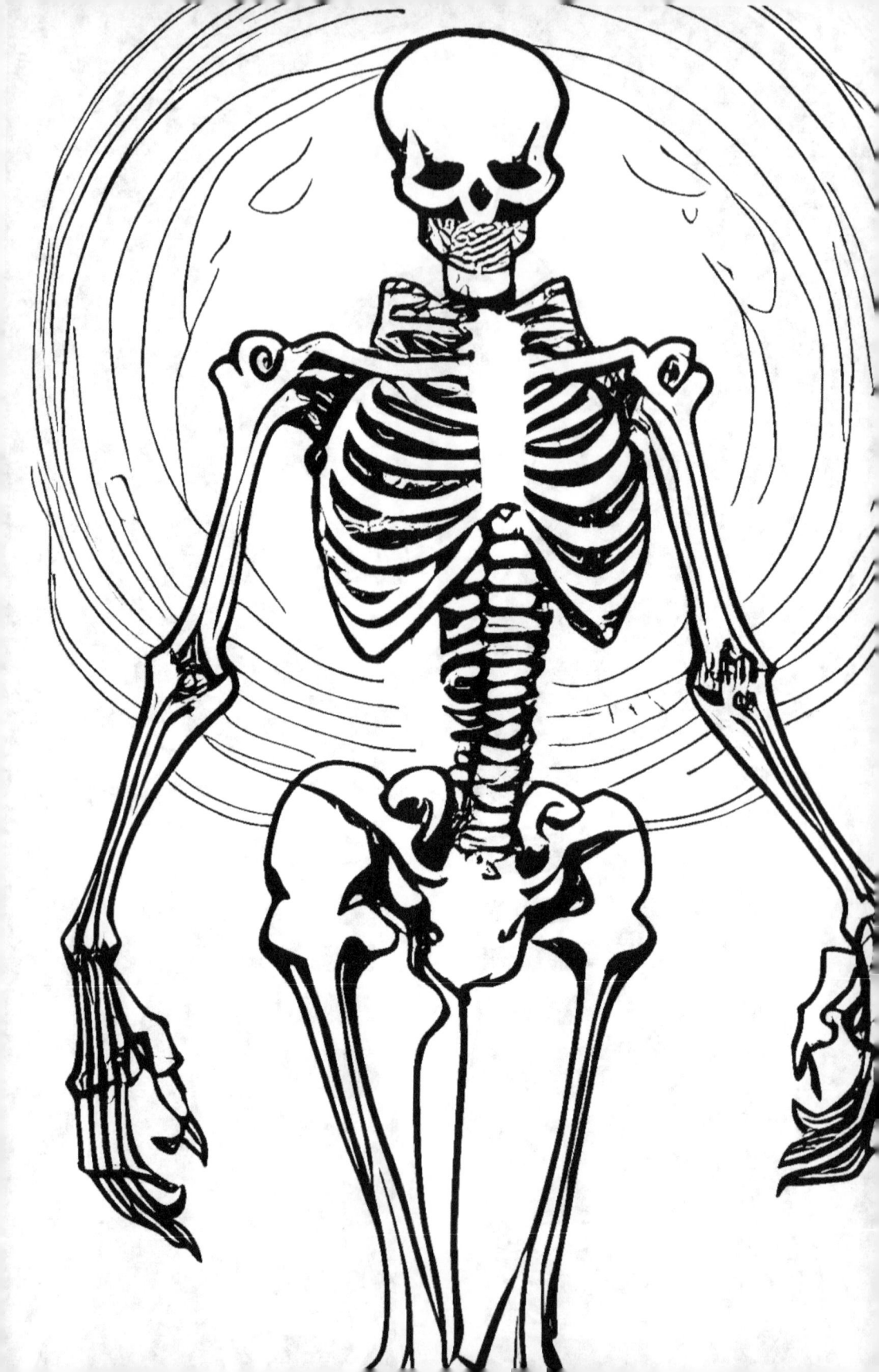

jeremyburt@ishopdailyonline.com jburt_01@hotmail.com
Make Money Online: https://ishopdailyonline.com
Print On Demand: https://ishopdaily.redbubble.com
Print On Demand @ Etsy: https://ishopdailyonline.etsy.com
dj12mind Instrumental Music Albums: https://dj12mind.com
Affiliate Products: https://index.ishopdailyonline.com
Patreon: https://www.patreon.com/user?u=80194438
Facebook: https://www.facebook.com/jeremy.burt2
Youtube:
https://www.youtube.com/channel/UCwV3nApPDh3dNHUGIX4w5nA
tiktok: https://www.tiktok.com/@jeremyburt4?lang=en
amazon: https://www.amazon.com/author/jeremyburt
THANK YOU FOR CHECKING IT OUT!

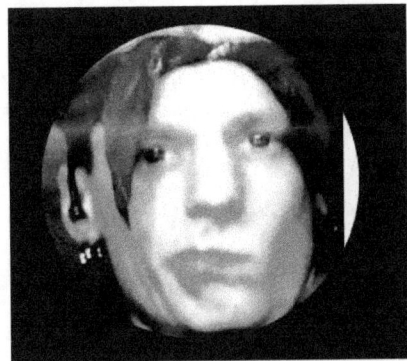

www.ingramcontent.com/pod-product-compliance
Lightning Source LLC
Chambersburg PA
CBHW070905220526
45466CB00005B/2139